Alan Spencer Hawkesworth

De Incarnatione Verbi Dei

Together with Three Essays Subsidiary to the Same

Alan Spencer Hawkesworth

De Incarnatione Verbi Dei
Together with Three Essays Subsidiary to the Same

ISBN/EAN: 9783337120191

Printed in Europe, USA, Canada, Australia, Japan

Cover: Foto ©Lupo / pixelio.de

More available books at **www.hansebooks.com**

De Incarnatione Verbi Dei

together with

Three Essays

subsidiary to the same

by the

Rev. Alan S. Hawkesworth

with a

Commendatory Preface

by the

Very Rev. E. A. Hoffman, S. T. D., LL. D.,
Dean of the Gen. Theo. Sem.

☦

ALBANY, N. Y.:
RIGGS PRINTING AND PUBLISHING CO.
1897

COPYRIGHT, 1897
BY
ALAN S. HAWKESWORTH

Essays by the same Author

☩

De Trinitate. *Price 15 Cents.*
   Formally commended by the Rt. Rev. G. F. Seymour, the Rt. Rev. H. C. Potter, and the Very Rev. E. A. Hoffman.

✟

On the Eucharistic Sacrifice and the Christian Priesthood. *Price 25 Cents.*
   Formally commended by the Rt. Rev. G. F. Seymour, the Rt. Rev. J. Scarborough, and the Very Rev. E. A. Hoffman.

✟

On Free Will. *Price 10 Cents.*

☩

The above can be obtained either of the publishers, or the **author.**

PREFACE

By the Very Revd. E. A. HOFFMAN, D.D., LL.D.
Dean of the Gen. Theo. Seminary.

 The doctrine of the Incarnation is not only the heart of the Gospel, but also the corner stone of the foundation on which rests the entire fabric of the Christian Faith. From it flows out all that gives vitality and strength to the Christian life. Apart from the Incarnation, which made possible and gave infinite value to the Atonement, the Christian disciple cannot look for the forgiveness of his sins, or for grace to walk in the path of God's commandments, or for hope of the world to come. "For God was in Christ, reconciling the world unto Himself, not imputing their trespasses unto them." And on it is built the entire system of work and worship, of faith and practice, which the Church was sent to proclaim and sustain in this evil world. "For other foundation can no man lay, than that is laid, which is Jesus Christ."

 Around it were arrayed the theories and errors which assailed the Faith in the early ages of the Christian Church, and compelled its adherents to set forth, for the instruction and protection of the faithful, the fuller and more explicit form of the Creed, known as the Nicene Creed. And strange as it may seem, many of these errors are being revived in our own days, under the veil of rationalistic and philosophical interpretations of the Scriptures. Most important, therefore, is it that the Church should be guarded against these errors by thorough instruction in this fundamental doctrine, for no one is safe who cannot give an intelligent account of the faith which is in him, and the ground on which it rests.

 I deem it no slight honour to be asked to write a word of preface to a Treatise which so ably states this doctrine as the Church has received the same. It gives a very admirable and comprehensive analysis of the doctrine in all its bearings and consequences. The work could well be used as the basis of a series of theological lectures, or as the framework of an exhaustive treatise; and the author has done an excellent work in preparing, and placing it within the reach of the clergy and laity. Without committing myself to all the statements contained in it, I heartily commend it to those who would be rightly instructed in the Christian Faith.

May God's blessing go with it, leading many who are bewildered by the strange doctrines, which in these days are set forth as the Gospel, to place their trust in the only Rock on which they can find rest and peace "Jesus Christ, the same yesterday and to-day, and forever."

E. A. HOFFMAN, D.D., LL.D.

ANALYTICAL SUMMARY

De Incarnatione Verbi Dei.

CHAPTER I.

The Incarnation, being the complement of all natural truths and ideals, in Nature, and in man; and that both individually, and racially; must also be, and is the vital heart of Christianity.

CHAPTER II.

Is, then, the Supreme Mystery; only comparable, even in a measure, to the incomprehensible "modification" that certainly took place at Prime Creation—"A priori" objections either "Deistic" or "Theological."—Their several consideration, and refutation. — The Incarnation a "local manifestation" — Illustrative analogies.

CHAPTER III.

Heretical theories considered, and confuted — Gnosticism, and Doketism — Arianism — Apollinarianism — Nestorianism — Eutychianism — Monophysitism — Theory of Gess, and Godet — Monothelitism — Adoptionism.

The Catholic doctrine of Chalcedon—The "Hypostatic Union"—The humanity "impersonal;" and, therefore, "never to be divided."

CHAPTER IV.

The Logos, being the "Archetypal Man," He, and He only, both could, and should be Incarnate in man—As He could not have been in an animal, or an angel.

The Virgin Birth, its necessity, nature, and "secretness."

CHAPTER V.

The "Kenosis," not an abrogation of Essence, but a "local limitation"—Our Lord's passibility, "ignorance," and growth—Yet His humanity perfect—And, therefore, inerrant, and impeccable—Relation of temptation to humanity, and its resistance—Christ, then, could be tempted; but could not sin—The "Two Wills" of our Lord.

CHAPTER VI.

Christ our "Example;" for He lived as "Very Man"—His Inspiration by the Holy Spirit—His prayers, and the several varieties of prayer—The Agony in Gethsemane; and Cry upon the Cross.

CHAPTER VII.

The Atonement, and its corporate nature—The "descent into Hell"—The estate of the dead—The Resurrection; and the "spiritual body."

CHAPTER VIII.

The Ascension, and Session—The Priesthood of our Lord, His gift of the Holy Spirit, His Church, and her Sacraments, all dependent on His Manhood. — The Incarnation, therefore, a primary intention, even apart from the "fall."

The Catholic doctrine of the Incarnation is, then, coherent and logical, and is also in agreement with all known facts—Some instances of this—Conclusion.

NOTE 14. ON THE "LOCAL MANIFESTATION.

Illustrative quotations from the Fathers and Schoolmen—Neglect of the doctrine of late years—"Communicatio idiomatum" a misleading phrase.

NOTE 31. ON THE HYPOSTATIC UNION IN CHRIST.

Distinction between the Trinitarian and the Christological "hypostasis."

THREE SUBSIDIARY ESSAYS

The Essential Nature of Sin.

Erroneous identification of "Sin" with "Sensuousness"—Leading to Dualism—And Buddhistic Nihilism—And again appearing in Puritanism.

Sin, not material, but spiritual—And is a "falling short," in spite of, and in opposition to Divine guidance—Is, therefore, illogical, hateful, and damning—Bearing of all this upon the doctrine of the Incarnation.

Spirit and Matter.

Theories concerning the inter-relation—Dualism—Materialism—Idealism—Pantheism.

The Catholic theory—"Matter" simply a "catena of phenomena"—But yet possesses an objective origin—Which origin we can only conceive of as "Spirit"—An analysis of our personality—The Ultimate Prime Origin, then, is the Absolute Spirit—Who must, at the least, be Personal.—Summary—Bearing of all this upon the doctrine of the Incarnation.

The Primary Criterion of Truth.

We can, and do know truth; not absolutely, but relatively.—For both our intellectual "prime data," and the testimonies of our senses, are, and must be valid—Objections to these statements refuted.

De Incarnatione Verbi Dei

CHAPTER I

THE glorious fact of the Incarnation—that the Logos of God took our nature upon Him, and became man,—this fact, I say, is not only the central and vital one of Christianity, differentiating it from all other faiths, and being the radiating source of all its teaching and Sacramental grace, but it is also the crown and complement to the truths of Natural Religion and Philosophy,—the point towards which they all tend, and in which, and in which alone, they find their satisfaction and fulfillment.

And this, indeed, must be so; for He, Who was there made manifest, is the Creator and Upholder of the Universe—the "Logos," in Whom "all things consist;"—and the being, therefore, and ultimate reason of all things, must, of necessity, so center in, and only be knowable through Him.

And yet furthermore: this inherence of all things in our Lord, as the "Logos," is not only theoretically, but also actually true; for the more closely we study the prime laws of being, both as we may observe them in Nature, and especially as we may learn them in the depths of our own individuality, and yet again discover them by observation in the souls of our fellowmen (thus proving them to be, not mere personal idiosyncrasies, but undoubtedly basic elements of humanity), the more closely, I say, we study these prime laws of being, the more will we also be struck by their (so to speak) incomplete and prophetic character; or in other words, by the testimony that they bear, if we will but hearken, to that Logos Who is ever Immanent in them, and Who has also been explicitly revealed to us as the Incarnate Christ of God.

Thus, considering first the vast Universe around us, we find everywhere the reign of order and of reason: all our science, all our knowledge, and our very capability for existence itself, is ultimately based upon this fundamental fact, namely that the world is no fortuitous and illogical chaos—a causeless "concourse of atoms;"—but is, on the contrary, an orderly and logical Cosmos, which we, as intelligent beings, are able, in some measure, to comprehend. To use, then, philosophical language, we may say that the underlying "noumena" of all things are "ideas," or λόγοι of God; which λόγοι, again, are ever grouped under wider and higher categories, until at last they finally center in Him Who is, in an especial manner, "the Supreme" Λόγος of God—the "Express Image" of the Father, and "First born of every creature."

Then, turning from this Cosmos around us to the depths of our own being, we again find this same centering in, and pointing upwards of our nature to Him : for we, each and all, philosopher, or savage, find both ourselves, and our fellows in general, to be possessed of certain primal intuitions, or axioms of truth —sensational, intellectual, moral, and religious ;—axioms that we have in no sense acquired, but have, on the contrary, universally inherited as the essential marks of our being.[1] Such, for instance, are those sensational axioms that give us the certainty of the existence of an external "Non-ego"—the Universe around us ;—such, again, are those axioms of intellectual truth —mathematical or logical,—that give us the capabilities of reasoning, and of knowledge ; and such, still again, are those axiomatical laws of the conscience, and those spiritual intuitions, that give us the truths of morality, and of Natural Religion.

Now all these axioms are, I repeat, innate and universal; and must therefore be accepted and used as undoubtedly true and valid, if we are to have any foundation, not only for our religion, or morality, or even for our thought, but also, as I have said, for our very existence itself.

And yet as we carefully study, as far as may be, these necessary and basic laws of our being, we are continually confronted with the fact that they are not complete in themselves—are not self-satisfied, and self explanatory,—but that they, equally with the "λόγοι" of Nature, point forward to an ideal knowledge and experience (i. e. of their "Logos") that ought to be, and must be attained. For the axioms of the intellectual, and even of the sensational nature, all demand a Great Prime Cause—a Creator and God of all;—and even more clearly do the instincts of the conscience, and of the spiritual intuitions, cry out for Him.

But if this be true of the individual soul, no less is it also true of the organic consciousness of our Race. For who, with the record of history before him, can deny that men, in all ages, have ever sought after their God—sought Him by religions and philosophies innumerable—sought Him through bitter agony and toil—sought Him, even despite of their ever present sense of their own sinfulness and of judgment—if only they might find Him for Whom their souls did yearn. The saying of St. Augustine "cor nostrum inquietum est donec requiescat in Te [Conf. lib. 1, cap. 1]," is, then, abundantly true ; and St. Philip

---

(1) That there are any such "prima data," and faculties for reasoning, inherited, and not personally acquired, is disputed by many psychologists; yet surely, in the first place, all reasoning, and therefore the acquiring of experience itself, necessitates some "*prime data*" for the mind ; and secondly, are not these "prima data"—these "innate powers"—the very qualities that give us, as I state in the text, our essential being itself? They are not, therefore, in any sense, *extra* gifts to the man, concerning the possession of which there might reasonably be doubts; but are rather the essential qualities of his Ego qua Ego. "Est Deus in nobis, agitante calescimus illo."

in his cry to the Christ, "Lord, show us the Father" (St. John, xiv, 8), was but voicing humanity's deepest need.

The knowledge, then, of God—the Great Father of all—is imperatively demanded, both by Nature, as its Creator and Reason, and by our own being, as our Enlightener and Guide; and yet that Father—that great Prime Cause of all,—because Primal and Infinite, must, in His Essence, be ever unknowable to man; and even in His relations to us as the Creator and Upholder of Nature, and of our own being, He can be but dimly and uncertainly apprehended; for our intellects are so finite, and our knowledge of things, necessarily, so partial and imperfect, that men have ever been tempted to think of their God, rather as an Irresistible Fatality, or even as an Irresponsible Despot, than as a loving *Father* of all.

As the Inspirer of our souls—the Logos-Giver of instinctive "light"—He can, it is true, be more freely and fully known; and that both because He is, in some measure, manifesting Himself to us therein as the True and the Holy; and is therefore, again, also more personally related to us. More personally related, I say, for His relation to us as the Creator is, evidently, more impersonal and non-individual in its character, than His relation to us as the Logos "Lightener" of our souls; for in the latter case we stand to Him rather as one taught does to his Teacher; but in the former case—or in creation—rather as a phenomenon (so to speak) does to its "Noumenal Reality" and Creator.

We can, then, know Him both more freely, and more fully, as the "Lightener and Inspirer" of our souls; and yet even this Divinity working in the soul, no less than the Divinity working in the world, can only be *certainly* known to man—can only, in other words, rise from being a mere philosophical theorem, to the place of an absolute and undoubted fact—by reason of that supreme revelation of our God, made to us in His Incarnation: for from that manifestation we first learn to think of Him, not so much as *Power* (for that we know before), nor yet as *Wisdom* (for that, too, Nature could teach us), but as *Love*, Tender and Infinite; and that is a lesson by no means clear from Natural Religion.

To use, then, the words of our Lord's reply to Philip "he that hath seen Me"—the Incarnate Logos of God—he, and he only, "hath seen the Father."

True, even before Christ came, men could, in some measure, feel and recognizing this Divine indwelling (vide Acts xiv, 17; and xvii, 27, 28); and were thereby, as I have said, moved to seek after Him, by their religions, and their philosophies, if haply they might find Him. Yet it was not, I repeat, until that supreme revelation of our God made to us in Christ, that men had any certain clue through the labyrinth of being; their philosophies, therefore, before that time, and still more their religions, were, at the best, but tentative, partial, and uncertain; and contained, even under the most favorable conditions, more or less of extraneous and hurtful admixture.²

But when Wisdom came unto His own, all that was best and purest in those heathen philosophies and religions—Pythagorean, Magian, Stoic, and Platonic—was fulfilled and completed in Him; so that the truly religious man, or philosopher, became now the true Christian, and brought the treasures of his wisdom to help unfold the Faith, even as the Magi brought their offerings to the cradle of their Lord. The heathen philosophies, in short, and philosophical religions, as the Fathers again and again insisted,³ bore the same relation to the Gentiles that the Mosaic dispensation bore to the Jews, in that they acted as "pedagogues" to lead men to, and prepare them for the Christ; this was their high office, and this their testimony to the Messiah Who should come.

And not only is all this theoretically true, but history, with its record of the preparation of mankind for, and their wonderful anticipations of that Advent, bears its subtle testimony to the same point, and shows us that Christianity was no mere afterthought—no illogical intrusion from without upon the Universe of God,—but that it was, in very truth, the Crown of the Ages—the ideal for which mankind had been preparing long before.

As, then, we study the heathen faiths, and heathen wisdom, we may well be struck, and perhaps even surprised, by their wonderful, even if fragmentary knowledge of the suffering Messiah Who should come. Thus we find in Classic Greece those intense longings for, and anticipations of an Incarnate Deliverer, which were, more or less clearly, voiced in the various "mysteries"—"Orphic," "Eleusinian," &c.; and which ran, like a fundamental chord, through the deepest tragedies of her poets. Such, again, were those expectations of a coming Deliverer and Restorer of the "Golden Age," universal in the Roman world of Augustus, and of which the famous "IV Eclogue" of Virgil is but a well known example. And such, yet again, were those Magian prophesies in Persia concerning the coming of "Soshyos,"

---

(2) In thus classing the Pre-Christian religions with philosophies, I need scarcely say that I by no means include in this category the Jewish Covenant [which was, I believe, properly a "Pre-Christian Christianity"]; but am merely referring to those great heathen faiths—such as Zoroastrianism, Brahminism, Buddhism, or Hellenism—that are, properly speaking, nothing else than the natural, if sometimes crude, expression of the philosophical and religious consciousness of the race, reaching out after God.

(3) Thus, to give two instances only, St. Augustine says [Retract: I, 13, 3.] "Res ipsa quae nunc Christiana religio nuncupatur, erat apud antiquos, nec defuit ab initio generis humani quousque ipse Christus veniret in carne, unde vera religio quae jam erat, coepit appellari Christiana." And St. Clement of Alexandria says ["Stromata." Book I, chap. V.] "Before the advent of the Lord philosophy was necessary to the Greeks for righteousness." * * * 'For God is the cause of all good things; but of some primarily, as the Old and New Testaments; and of others by consequence, as philosophy. Perchance, though, philosophy was given to the Greeks directly and primarily, till the Lord should call the Greeks. And thus was a schoolmaster to bring the Hellenic mind, as the Law the Hebrew, to Christ." Vide also chap. xvi; and Book VI, chaps. v, vi, viii, xvii. &c.

With all this agrees St. Paul's appeal to the natural religious consciousness in Acts xiv. 15-17, and xvii. 22-31, as already quoted, and especially the reference on "Mar's Hill" to "one of your poets" as a *prophetic* or *religious* authority. And, in fact, how could it well be otherwise; unless, indeed, Christianity were an *unnatural* religion, foisted in upon the revolting mind.

or " Honofer "—the Incarnate " Word,"—Who should both redeem mankind, and unite them with Himself.

In short, whatever part, or period we study of the pre-Christian world, we find these prophecies, and anticipations of the Christ Who should come; from Egypt to Scandinavia, from India or China to the Celts of the West, even in pre-Christian America—Mexico and Peru—we everywhere find, I repeat, this dim foreknowledge of Him.

When the Angels, then, sang over Bethlehem, on that first Christmas morn, it was over the supreme mystery of humanity—the revelation in flesh of Him towards Whom all the lines of our being, personal and racial, converge; and in Whom, and in Whom alone, they find their satisfaction and fulfillment.

But the Incarnation of the Logos being, thus, the crown and complement of all natural truth, it evidently must also be, as I have said, the central and vital fact of Christianity—its differential and causal doctrine, and the well spring of all its teaching and grace.

For the essential doctrine of Christianity—that which makes it *Christianity*—is, manifestly, not in its ethical teaching; nor in the truths it teaches concerning man's being and nature, and the immortality of his soul; nor, yet again, in the truths of our Creator's Being and Essence—even of His Triune Nature,—and His government of the world; and that because these truths are part of the religious " prime data " inspirational in the heart of every man, as man (vide note 1 page 2); and therefore belong rather to " Natural Religion ": this being so, then Christianity, evidently, only possesses these truths in common with all other faiths; and can, therefore, in short, only especially claim them as establishing and making them certain, or in other words, as lifting them out of the category of more or less tentative beliefs, into that of basic and undoubted facts.

But it is the truth that both completes and interweaves all these "natural" truths of the Being of God, and the being of man—namely the truth of the Incarnation of God in man—that is, as I have said, both the differential and causal doctrine of the Christian Faith, and the plenary fountain head of all its teachings and Sacramental grace. For it is, evidently, from this prime fact, and it alone, that the subsidiary facts of our Lord's life—such as His Atonement, Resurrection, and Ascension—derive all their meaning and validity; and it is also this fact, as I will hereafter show, that underlies and gives significance to both our Lord's gift of the Holy Spirit to His Church, and that Church's Sacramental system as a whole—her claim of Commission from her Head, her Priesthood, Baptisms, and Eucharists, and the Gospel of Redemption that she preaches to the world.

Thus the Incarnation of our Lord is, if we may use the simile, like a gold ring, *to* which all the truths of our nature converge, *in* which they are made secure, and *from* which, in turn, radiate all the special doctrines of our most Holy Faith.

CHAPTER II

THE Incarnation, then, in man of the Logos of God is, as I have shown, the crown and necessary complement of all natural truths, as it is also the living and vivifying heart of Christianity; and yet, because it is this supreme and central truth, it is also (as, indeed, might be expected) the most deeply mysterious of all; so that, from the very first preaching of the Faith, men—believers, as well as unbelievers—have not ceased to wonder and surmise how, in reality, God could become man.

"The Incarnation of the Logos of God!" Surely, as we say these words, and endeavor to realise, in some slight degree, their import, we can well stagger at the tremendous meaning they convey. For what else in human history—even the fall of empires, or of nations—can compare, for one moment, with such an event? One that is certainly the greatest, not only that humanity, or this earth, but that the Universe itself has ever seen. For this Incarnation of the Logos is, surely, speaking with all solemnity and reverence, a stupendous and all important event in the Being of the Godhead Himself—even, in some sense, a *modification* of His previous existence,—affecting profoundly, not only the Logos, but also the Father, in Whose Bosom He is, and the Holy Spirit, Who Eternally deriveth Plenitude from the Father through Him.

There is, then, we may say, but one other event that can be even faintly comparable to this incomprehensible "*modification*" in the Divine Existence, and that is in the apparent, and yet again incomprehensible "*modification*" that took place at the beginning of the Creation of God. This, I say, was certainly an apparent "modification," for a previously non-existent Universe was then brought into actual being, and became, in brief, an entity that was, and is, in some real sense, external to, and distinct from, its Creator and God. And that there *was* this beginning—that this external Universe is *not* eternally existent,—is, I think, evident from the following lines of thought.

In the first place we have the empirical evidence of our senses that all things in the Cosmos are transient, and temporary; and therefore must once have had a beginning; and still further our sciences of physical phenomena—our geology, physics, astronomy, etc.,—all assure us that there was a time when this world was not; and if not this world, then presumably neither the Universe.

And these conclusions are still further enforced by the following philosophical arguments. If the Universe be thought eternally existent, then it must also be thought either self existent, or else a necessary production from the Eternal God.

But if we hold it to be *self existent* apart from God, then it must itself be a God;[4] and we are thus driven either to a theory of *two* mutually exclusive Infinities (which is absurd); or else to a theory of an Infinity consisting in an atheistic Universe (the deductions from which are equally absurd); and as we may further add, under either of these suppositions, whether it be that of a self existent world with a self existent God, or that of a self existent world alone, any change or decay, such as our senses give us cognisance of, would be utterly and entirely incongruous.

But on the other hand, if the Universe be thought to be a *necessary production* from God (as Pantheism teaches), then we would have something that would be, not a finite creation of God, but (in theological language) rather something that would be best described as an "Infinite Logos," *Begotten* of His Essence; and therefore also something that would be, in a sense, "ὁμοούσιος" with Him, and be God; and ought, then, to be worshipped as Him; while in this case, again, the observed change and decay in Nature would be utterly incompatible.

So, then, both from empirical, and philosophical considerations we are sure that the Universe is not eternal, but once began to be; yet this, I say, entails upon us the recognition of an incomprehensible "modification," at the moment of prime creation, in the existence of the Eternal One.

And this is true, even if we adopt the apparently tenable idea, advocated by some eminent theologians, that although the actual entity of the Universe had a definite beginning, yet the *ideals* of that entity had no such beginning, but were eternally pre-existent in the Divine Logos; for even granting this as probably true, yet the *"preciptation"* (so to speak) of the Universe of God, from its eternally pre-existent ideality, to its finite, created, and historical existence, was certainly, I repeat, an apparent, although incomprehensible "modification" in the Being of the Eternal. Before that time He was all in all; but since that time He has, in a real and true sense, been self limited by His world—has, in short, given it *EX-istence*, where previously was only *SUB-sistence* in Him.

Thus although the Infinite Godhead is, by His very Essence, the Everlasting and Unchangeable, yet still we have this incomprehensible, yet none the less evident, "modification" of existence and relation in that Unchangeable.

But even this wonder of Creation, great as it is, manifestly falls far short of that supreme wonder of all—the Incarnation. Nay! it is even, as I have shown, in relation to the "λόγοι" of the Universe, an entirely subsidiary fact, centering upon, leading up to, and preparing for, that great Central Mystery.

The Incarnation, then, being this stupendous antinomy—this

---

(4) And, as St. Athanasius further argues [De Incar; Verbi Dei § 2. 4.] God would then be, not a *creator* [κτίστης], but a mere *artizan* [τεχνίτης], working with pre-existent material.

(5) This argument from change has already been mentioned among the empirical evidences; but yet it, manifestly, has also a place here.

"modification" in the Unchangeable—although an antinomy that is, in some degree, paralleled and illustrated by an only less stupendous one, namely Creation itself, it ought not to greatly surprise us if men, now as ever, feel some difficulty in realising and believing in that supreme Wonder; and in truth, if we do *not* find this feeling of difficulty, and perhaps even of doubt, it will, in most cases, be only because they have never fairly considered it, and are either stupid and thoughtless, or else careless and indifferent.

Let us, then, as briefly, and yet as clearly and accurately as may be, endeavor to explain, and show the logical sequences of the Church's doctrine of the Incarnation. But as to her beliefs in matters of fact—namely that the Logos *was* so Incarnate, that Jesus of Nazarath was that Incarnate Logos, and the various events in His Blessed Life and Teaching,—all these will not be expounded in this present treatise; unless, indeed, it be in the way of passing and necessary reference; and that for two reasons.

In the first place, it is "imprimis" necessary to demonstrate that this doctrine of the Incarnation is logically coherent and possible, before any arguments can be validly advanced as to its actual existence in fact; for any "proofs" derived from history, human testimony, or internal evidence can only avail to establish something that is, at least, not "a priori" incredible.

And in the second place, experience will also, I think, show us that it is precisely in this direction of supposed "a priori" incredibility that the doubts and difficulties of the majority, if not all, of the stumblers at this doctrine lie.

Let us, then, I repeat, take the Church's doctrine of the Incarnation—that doctrine that is to her, as I have said, the center and foundation of all her faith and ritual,—and showing the logical coherence and reasonableness of it, thereby strengthen the hands of our brethren; and also, in so doing, provide the necessary primary foundation for any historical argument as to the facts of the Gospel narrative.

To begin, then, it may be said that the "a priori" objections to the Incarnation may all be summed up under two chief heads, first what I may call the class of "Deistic" objections, and secondly what, for want of a better term, I may term the "theological" class.

First, then, as to the "Deistic" objections. Men, for many ages past, have pointed to the mighty Universe around us, with all its evidences of o'erwhelming wisdom and power, and have asked how it could be possible, or credible, that the Creator and God of all should so condescend as to come into this petty world of ours, and be born as a man among men?

This objection is as old as Christianity itself; and, as derived from the old Epicurean Deism, was one of the first difficulties raised by the philosophers of Greece and Rome. It was, again, especially congenial to the Deists of the last century; and although Deism, as a philosophy, is now dead, yet the objection is still advanced; our greatly developed acquaintance with both the vastness, and the intricacy of Nature being supposed, by some, to have even increased its force.

And yet all that is necessary to abundantly expose its sophistry is to bring forward a very elementary theological and philosophical axiom, namely, that God is necessarily Infinite and Absolute,—not merely "magni-finite" (to coin a new word) as Deism supposes,—and is therefore *omnipresent* at *all* times to *all* His Creation. This simple, and yet most effective reply is again as old as Christian theology itself; and was powerfully urged by the great St. Athanasius himself, in refutation of this very objection to the Incarnation, namely, that "God was too great." [6]

It is, in fact, only so long as Deistic habits of thought prevail, and God is anthropomorphically pictured as a kind of magnified emperor, utterly dissevered from, and outside of His Creation—a Creation, it is true, that had once been formed by the "Great Artizan"[7] in the past; but yet one that had been then abandoned by Him to take care of itself; while He rarely, if ever, interfered with its working; and then only capriciously—it is, I say, only while this strange type of thought prevails that men can think of God as "too great" to care for His Universe; and as, certainly, "too great" to become Incarnate in man.

But this, let it be noticed, is an entirely anthropomorphic conception of the Godhead—an ascribing to Him of our faults, finite limitations, and imperfections,—and not merely an anthropometric one—or a conceiving of Him, it is true, in a necessarily manlike way; but yet in the terms of our highest perfections and knowledge.

Certainly *all* our conceptions, not merely in theology, but in every department of thought, are, and must be anthropometric[8]—or in a "man's manner,"—for we, manifestly, can only think in the terms of a man's mind: but we need not, and ought not to be anthropomorphic—or project our "$μορφή$," or "estate" into Nature, and its God; and read therein all our imperfections and limitations—for this is a type of thought that is possible only to savage, or shallow minds.

Deistic and anthropomorphic conceptions, then, of the "greatness of God," and His want of concern for the world, although possible to the shallow Eighteenth century, or to decadent Greece and Rome, are quite impossible to us now. Scientific

---

(6) St Athanasius [De Incar: Verbi Dei, § 41.] "The Philosophies of the Greeks say that the Universe is a great body, and rightly so. For we see it, and its parts are objects of our senses. If, then, the Word of God is in the Universe, which is a body, and has united Himself with the whole, and with all its parts, what is there surprising or absurd, if we say that He has united Himself with man also?"

(7) Such was the title that Voltaire, and the other 18th century Deists, gave to God! But compare the words of St. Athanasius quoted in note 4, and also what is said on pp. 6 and 7, concerning the dependence of the Universe on God.

(8) I have coined this word, and differentiated between it and "anthropomorphic," in the interests of clearness and accuracy; for the latter term has too long been used in both the "morphic" and the "metric" senses, with a resultant obscurity and confusion of thought.

knowledge is ever giving us a more vivid realisation of the living Unity of Nature—teaching us, in other words, that it is, not so much a machine, as an organism;—and we, therefore, can now only conceive of God as did the wisest philosophers of old, and the ancient Fathers of the Church; namely, not as a magnified emperor, remote from His Creation, but as the Omnipresent and Infinite "Reality" of the Universe—the Ultimate Soul of all.[9]

The deepest thought, then, has ever found its most perfect analogy for this relation of the Creator to His Cosmos, in the relation that exists between the body and soul of man, that sole "manifestation" and "reality"—"phenomenon," and "noumenon"—of which we have any certain knowledge;[10] and if it be objected that this, not less than the Deism exposed above, is only a delusive projection of our own being into Nature, we may reply by making the distinction already noted, and saying that while it is certainly anthropometric—or a reading of Nature and Being through the eyes of a man, and an interpreting it in the terms of our highest and most perfect categories,—yet it certainly is not, like Deism, anthropomorphic—or a reading of ourselves, with all our frailties and imperfections, into the Universe and into God.

Nor, again, is this truth of the Immanence of God in His World at all incongruous, as some, perchance, may imagine it to be, with what I have already said (pp. 6 and 7) concerning the real separateness that exists between Him and that world.

We certainly know that there is this separateness, and that we, for example, are not God; and that both from primary innate truth, and (so far as may be) from experience also; no theory, therefore, or deductions, philosophical or religious, can ever be allowed to contradict this primary fact of our being; and any theory that does so, is thereby self condemned.

If, then, this analogy between God and His Cosmos, on the one hand, and the spirit and body of man, on the other, if, I say, it did so imply the identity, or confusion of God and His Cosmos, then it would be manifestly untrue. But it does not make this flagrant blunder; for in the analogy chosen—i. e., the spirit and body of man,—the two terms, while certainly closely interconnected (as, again, God and His creation must be) are not, by any means, to be confused, or identified. Under this Catholic and philosophical conception, then, of God as the "Soul of the Universe," which is the highest and most perfect conception we are capable of forming, we are able to think of that Universe as *existing*, it is true; but yet not as *self existing*, apart from, and dissevered from Him, Who is its Sole Ultimate "Reality."

If this were not true—if, in other words, the Universe were

---

(9) Vide St. Paul's words in Acts xvii, 25-28; and Coloss: I, 17; &c.
(10) For this statement, and the succeeding paragraph, see the Essay on "Spirit and Matter."

not God's "Body"—then its self existence would, as has been already shown (pp. 6 and 7), imply also its eternity, andt herefore its essential equality with, and independence of God. But, Nature being the "Body of God," the smallest atom exists because, and only because, He is ever its Thinker and Upholder; and thus is *ever giving* (not *has* given) it existence in Him.

In short, this wonderful Immanence of God in Nature necessarily implies also His Transcendence; or, in other words, just as I am able to be immanent in my body, and to give it existence, because, and only because, I am greater than my body—because I am a living entity, a spiritual, individual, and thinking unit,—so God is able to "think" His Universe, and give it real existence, because, and only because, He is Infinite and Absolute Transcendent Wisdom and Power. Pantheism, then, in not recognising this fact, makes the same terrible mistake with respect to God, that Materialism makes with respect to man; for as the latter seeks to explain away the essential unity of our personality—the spirit and the reason—as being merely the sum total of diverse, and often opposite "sensations," so too the former endeavors to similarly explain away the Personality, the Unity, the Transcendence, and the Reason of God, and predicates Him simply as the sum total—"$το παν$"—of all the diverse, and often opposite "laws," and "forces" of the Universe. The same stricture, therefore, applies with equal force to both of these systems; "laws," "forces," "sensations;" what possible meaning, we may well ask, or existence have they, unless it be in relation to a *pre-existent* Being—God, or man, as the case may be—of Whom they are the "laws," the "forces," or the sensations?"[11]

But yet the truth that Pantheism does, in a measure, see, and which Catholic theology more fully sees, and insists upon as fundamental, and yet again, the truth upon which all modern science is, more or less, consciously based, namely the Unity of Nature as a whole, and the Immanence of the Creative Logos in it, this truth, I say, is sufficient to show the utter futility of the Deistic objection that "God is too great" to become Incarnate in man. For if He be the "Omnipresent Soul", "giving to all life, and breath, and all things"—giving existence to each atom as fully as to each world,— then truly nothing can be either "small" or "great" with Him; and we can well plead the argument of St. Athanasius already mentioned (vide note 6), and ask what is there incredible in He, Who is in all things, making a more perfect manifestation of Himself through one?

Deistic objections, then, to the Incarnation, based on the "greatness of God", are mistaken and invalid; and yet the very conception of the Godhead that shows their untenableness, gives rise to the second difficulty, namely what I have called, for want of a better name, the "theological" one: although this, as

---

(11) On all the foregoing discussion compare also the Essay on "Spirit and Matter."

I trust I can show, is only because the doctrine of the Incarnation is not correctly apprehended.

In other words, so long as the Blessed Trinity is falsely conceived of in a Tritheistic (or rather, to coin a more exact term, in a *Trideistic*) way, then it is, of course, quite possible to imagine One of these Gods as leaving the other Two in heaven, and becoming a man. But let the true and Catholic doctrine of the Trinity be clearly apprehended, namely that God is, not Three, but One in Three Personalities—Father, Son, and Holy Spirit,— then, I say, it becomes at once incredible that One Personality of the Trinity—namely the Logos—should, so to speak, "dethrone" Himself, forsake the Unity, and descend to earth as a man!

This would be simply inconceivable, even if it were only in relation to His Cosmic functions; for in that Logos all things, as I have shown, "consist", or in other words, have their actual existence; and if He, then, should, for one single instant, cease to be the Logos, and to give them being, then they also, at the same instant, would necessarily cease to exist.

But if this "dethronement" of the Logos is inconceivable in relation to the Universe, still less, if possible, is it conceivable in relation to the Essence of God; that One Personality of the Trinity should, for a moment, be wanting—that the Logos should cease, even for a time, to be the Ever Begotten of the Father, and the Eternal Giver of Plenitude to the Holy Spirit, Who Ever Proceedeth through Him—all this, I say, is simply utterly incredible.[12]

Here then we have the "theological" difficulty in conceiving of the Incarnation, a difficulty, it will be noticed that springs not, like the first objection, from a false and Deistic conception of the Godhead, but rather from a true and vital grasp upon the Catholic doctrine of the Trinity.

And this difficulty is all the more potent in fact in that there are many earnest believers who, even if not consciously, are yet subconsciously oppressed and injured by it. They may not be able to clearly and articulately formulate the difficulty; yet it is nevertheless, as I have said, subconsciously present to them; and especially so in their endeavors to obtain a fairly coherent picture of our Lord's character and work; but this they find themselves unable to attain; for their conceptions of Him, as a

---

(12) Yet, strange to say, this hypothesis has actually been broached by Zinzendorf, Thomasius [Christi Person und Werk], Gess [Die Lehre von der Person Christi], Ebrard[Christliche Dogmatik], and Godet [Com: on the Gospel of St. John]; the latter, and Gess, even predicating a "depotentiation" of the Logos to an utterly unconscious germ; which germ, on becoming a man, only attained, or rather recovered, complete self consciousness by years of patient experience (vide page 21). And furthermore ; while this self consciousness was being thus slowly recovered, the Father, and the Holy Spirit are represented as carrying on by Themselves the work of the Godhead; so that the Trinity, in short, for a season, became only a Duality!!

Surely all this is a most extraordinary hypothesis; and is only conceivable, even for an instant, to a thorough going "*Trideist*;" or in other words, to one who conceives of the Blessed Trinity not merely, in a heretical manner, as Three Gods, but also in an eighteenth century fashion, as Three *Deistic* Gods—three gigantic men;— each utterly separate, both from his fellows, and from the world over which he jointly presides!!

man, and as the Logos, are mutually incongruous, and ever contradictory ideals. This unfortunate hiatus leads, then, to one or the other aspect of our Lord's character, and generally that of His Logos Nature, being lost sight of, and practically, at any rate, denied; and hence arises false and heretical thought, corrupting and injuring the whole Christian life.

And yet there need not be this formidable difficulty, if we will but approach the subject in a clear and accurate manner. Thus, in the first place, it is clearly unimaginable that the Logos should, at any time, even for one moment, cease to be the Logos; this is plainly evident, as already has been shown, both from the Being of God, and the Being of the Universe.

And still further, the Generation of the Logos from the Father, and the Procession of the Holy Spirit from the Father through Him, are, as the Creed confesses, *Eternal* in their character; and it is hardly necessary to add that this does *not* mean at an "infinitely remote date in the past"; but on the contrary, a Generation and Procession that is *now, as ever, taking place*, arising from the Very Being of God.

The Incarnation of the Logos, then, does not, and cannot mean, I repeat, that He ceased, even for a time, to be the Logos —or was, in other words, "dethroned";—but, on the contrary, simply means that He was, during that Incarnation, *locally manifested* (1 Timothy, iii, 16,), and as I will hereafter show, also *locally limited* by the manhood He then assumed.

To elucidate my meaning; nearly all men will acknowledge that at certain times and places God has wrought in a special manner through certain "inspired" men—poets, teachers, or heroes.— Christians, furthermore, will hold that this Divine power has been manifested in a yet more signal manner through His Church—her saints, her doctors, and her councils,—and more especially through "inspired" writers—Moses and the Prophets, under the Old Dispensation; the Apostles and Evangelists under the New.

Here, then, in all these instances of "Inspiration," whether it be that of a lower, or a higher type—the "Inspiration," of a poet, of a saint, or of an Evangelist,—we have yet clear instances of a "manifestation" of God, *localised* and even *limited* by the personality and limitations of the man Whom He thus "inspires;" and yet assuredly a "local manifestation and limitation" that, in no sense, and in no way, conflicts with His Eternal Omnipresence and Omnipotence.

But we can go even further than this in our analogies; for there is, if we will but see it, a "local and limited" manifestation" of God, in a real and true sense, immanent in the heart of every man, namely in that instinctive illumination of "prime data"—sensational, intellectual, moral, and religious,—to which

---

(13) See pp. 41-43 on the necessary limitations of instinctive guidance and light.

I have already referred. Thus St. John, in the opening of his Gospel (St. John, i, 9), tells us that the Logos is "the Light that lighteneth *every* man that cometh into the world;" and with this agree both St. Paul's words at Lystra (Acts xiv, 17), and at Athens (Acts xvii, 28), and the constant teaching of the Catholic Church. And who, in truth, in considering both in history, and their own souls, that inspirational knowledge of, and thirst for God, of which I have already spoken (pp. 2 and 3), and especially noting those wondrous twin "lights" of conscience and intellectual truth—"lights" that are, to a large degree, impersonal and non-individualised in their character,—inherent in man, as man (vide note 1), and ever guiding him onward to righteousness, truth, and God, who, I say, in considering these things can fitly deny them to be real "inspirational" guidings from God? Here, then, again we have another clear instance, as I have said, of a local and limited "manifestation" of God; a "manifestation" that is immanent in each individual heart; and yet One that is not the less Omnipresent to all His Creation.

And here "en passant" I may remark that this "local manifestation" of the Logos in every man, or in other words, this verity that every human being, as such, is a temple of the indwelling Light, this, I say, is the fact that gives us the key to both the modicum of truth in, and the vast fallacy of, the "liberal" quibble that "Christ was, no doubt, an Incarnation of God, for so is every man."

True, every man *is*, as I have shown, in some sense, a "manifestation" of God; and so too, in a higher sense, is every hero, poet, and sage; and so again, in a yet higher sense, is every saint, every Father of the Church, and the Church herself as a whole; and in an even still higher sense may we say that the "inspired" Apostles and Prophets of God are "manifestations" of Him.

But yet the Incarnation of the Logos differs from all the foregoing, not only in degree, but in kind; for an "Incarnation," as I will show, means something far surpassing mere possession, even though that be of the fullest possible kind. The accurate meaning of "Incarnate" in short, is for God, not merely to be *in* a man, but to *be* a man; and that is a wonder of which we have no exemplar, apart from Christ.

It must not, then, be overlooked or forgotten that all the "possessions" mentioned above—of a man, a hero, a Christian, or an Evangelist—are merely examples of a *local manifestation* and *limitation* of the Omnipresent and infinite; and are not, in any sense, analogues that can be pressed beyond that point.

But using them for this, and this purpose only, we may say that we can thus obtain a clear conception of the "local manifestation" of our Lord: a conception that, while it guards the reality of the Incarnation, yet leaves inviolate the Catholic doctrine of the Godhead; and one, moreover, that is hinted at in a saying of our Lord's (St. John, iii, 13); and as such, has been more or less fully unfolded by the ancient Fathers of the Church.[14]

In the Incarnation, then, of our Lord, He, as the Logos, never ceased, for one instant, or in any place, to be Omnipresent; but the Presence, invisible elsewhere, was visible within the limits of the human body of the Christ.

---
(14) Vide the note at the end of this treatise, on the "Local Manifestation."

CHAPTER III

LET us now pass on to consider, as far as may be, how in truth our Lord became man; and it will, I think, help us if we first lay down how He did *not;* or, in other words, if we consider, and refute, as briefly as possible, the various heretical teachings upon this vital point.

To begin then, and passing by Ebionitism, which, in stating that our Lord was a man *only*, denied any Incarnation at all, we may say that the succession of heretical doctrine on this point, both logically and historically, is as follows.

There were first those various heresies, included under the generic term of "Gnostic," which were, strictly speaking, non-Christian in origin, anti-Christian in many respects, and in fact were the only slightly modified presentations of ancient Syrian philosophies.[15] Nevertheless inasmuch as the "Æon Christ" was given a place in all their systems, and they all professed to have a Christology, it may be well to briefly notice their wide divergence from the Church's doctrine.

Starting, then, as they did, from the fundamental principal of the essential evil of "matter," quâ "matter," and the equally essential good of "spirit," quâ "spirit," it is, of course, manifest that no real Incarnation of Christ could be allowed; the apparent humanity of our Lord was, then, explained away in various fashions. Some, like Cerinthus, predicated a mere "possession," or inspiration by the "Æon Christ" of the man Jesus; which "possession" was supposed to have commenced at His baptism, and to have ceased at His crucifixion. This theory re-appears, in a somewhat modified form, in the later, and more properly Christian heresies of Nestorianism, and Adoptionism, and will be considered and confuted in those connections.

Others, again, of the Gnostics conceived of our Lord as indeed the "Æon Christ," and Him alone; but avoided the fancied corruption of the Divine Spirit by a material body, by predicating to that material body a merely illusionary existence. True, said they, He *appeared* to possess a material body, and to live the life of a man; but it was in appearance only; for that an "Emanation" from the Divine—an "Æon"—could be bound by a body, could hunger, could suffer, and above all could be crucified and die, this, to them, was utterly inconceivable. All the accounts, therefore, in the Gospels, of such a manhood, and such a death, were to be taken as being merely subjective illusions, having no real foundation in fact; for our Lord's body was, in short, to all intents and purposes, a phantasm—an apparition—and nothing more. This is the strange theory named

---

(15) Vide the Essay on the "Essential Nature of Sin," re the "Gnostics."

by the Church the "Doketic" one, and sternly repudiated by her as subversive of all truth and reality. How, it was well asked, if such a theory were correct, was He properly Incarnate at all? And furthermore, if His life and His death were thus mere figments, must not our redemption be a figment also; and finally was not the Holy and True One thereby made the Author and Father of lies!!

Yet another strange Gnostic idea, closely connected with Doketism, was that our Lord's humanity came direct from heaven, and that He took no substance of His mother, but passed through her "tanquam per canalem."[16] This, probably, at first, was only intended as an expression of His body's phantasmal unreality; but the later Gnostics (such as Valentinus), and the Manichæans, seem to have taken it in a more literal sense; and it was, strangely enough, said to have even found a place in the semi-doketic system of the Christian Apollinarius. From the Manichæans it passed over, probably by way of the Paulicians, to various of the heretical sects of the Middle Ages; and was part of the heretical inheritance of the abhorred Anabaptists.

Leaving these unreal and fanciful systems we pass on to the consideration of the great Arian heresy, in so far as it affected the doctrine of the Incarnation. The Christology of this sect, with its semi-gnostic principles,[17] does not seem to have been very clearly defined; but from all the indications that we can gather it was probably of an Apollinarian and semi-gnostic type. The hyper-angelic, semi-divine, *Emanated* "Son" was conceived of as inhabiting a human body to which He was both "Ego" and mind;[18] and furthermore *sin* was held to be an essential quality of finite and created wills; so that the "Son," although hyper-angelic, being yet created, could and must, therefore, be chargeable with sin. The dualistic theory of "sin" that this implies will be examined in an Essay upon the "Essential Nature of Sin" following this treatise; at present we need only consider the Christology; and this can more conveniently be done by taking up its next, and more Christian type.

Apollinarius, the quondam friend of St. Athanasius, fought bravely against the Arian misbelief; but, unfortunately, in so doing, assumed that both the Arian Christology, and theory of

---

(16) "Χριστὸν υἱὸν ἴδιον ,'ἀλλὰ και ψυχικόν" . . . "εἶναι δὲ τοῦτον ,τον διὰ Μαρίας διοδεύσαντα καθάπερ ὕδωρ διὰ σωλῆνος ὁδεύει." [St. Irenaeus Contra Haer: Lib; I, cap. 7, § 2.]

(17) The underlying Gnostic principles of Arianism, on the one hand, and the widespread influence, at the time, of such Dualistic theories, on the other, are often not as clearly apprehended as they should be; and the consequence is that the exceedingly rapid, even if short lived, successes of Arianism are wondered at as inexplicable. But the truth is that much of the Pre-Christian, and Non-Christian Greek thought was fundamentally Dualistic in its character Arianism, therefore, with its *Emanational* theory of Christ, was most agreeable to the peculiar intellectual atmosphere of its age; and as such, both reaped all the accruing popularity and advantage; and was also correspondingly evanescent.

(18) "Σῶμα γὰρ αὐτον [i. e. τον Λόγον] 'ἄψυχον ἔφη [Ἄρειος] εἰληφέναι, ἐνηργηκέναι δὲ τὰ τῆς ψυχῆς τὴν Θεότητα." [Theodoret Haer: Fab: Lib: IV, cap. 1.] Vide also Epiphanius [Adv: Haer: Lib: II; Haer: LXIX, cap. 19.

"sin," were practically correct. They had objected to the Godhead of Christ on the ground that He "did not know," and was also, as man, necessarily passable and peccable, things that were clearly impossible to the Infinite and Eternal God.

To all this Apollinarius rightly replied by denying our Lord's peccability; but, at the same time, he unfortunately granted to the Arians their contention that *sin* was an essential property of a real humanity—that faultiness, in short, was not merely an accident, and a "fall," but was, on the contrary, an inherent quality in every created will;—[19] thus distinctly approximating, in this respect, to the Gnostic "evilness of matter."

Under the pressure of this theory of the evilness "per se" of humanity, he could, indeed, allow to our Lord a human *body*; but he was forced to deny the existence of a human *mind* and *will*. The Logos, in short, was pictured as abiding in a human-appearing shell, of which He was, not only the "Ego," but the rational mind as well: and it was in relation to this "shell" theory that he was said to have even adopted the "tanquam per canalem" heresy spoken of above.[20]

Catholics naturally replied that all this was only the Doketic "illusionary" heresy in a mere modified form: He, Who was the God of truth, would not condescend to such a lie; and moreover, such a false simulacrum of humanity would eviscerate of all real meaning both His Incarnation, and the Redemption He had made.

And even still further: such a negation of any real humanity to our Lord, other than His mere physical existence, would render utterly meaningless, not only the mental anguish He endured in the Garden, and on the Cross, but above all, and especially, His "descent into Hell" after death; for obviously, on the one hand, our Lord's human *body* did not so "descend," but lay in the sepulchre; while, on the other hand, in His Godhead He could not properly be said to have "descended;" inasmuch as any such notion of change of locality is entirely debarred by His Essential Omnipresence. Our Lord, therefore, could be said to "descend into Hell," simply and only, in His Incarnate relation as *man*; which relation, again, or "manhood," can, obviously, only consist in that element of His humanity—namely, "mind," and "vital life"—which was not resting in the Syrian tomb: this is, evidently, an all conclusive objection to Apollinarianism; and as such it was advanced, and accepted at the time.[21]

But if Apollinarianism was mere modified Doketism, the next heresy was but a modified Cerinthian Gnosticism, in its doc-

---

(19) Vide St. Athanasius [De Incar. contra Apoll. Lib: I, § 2], who quotes him as saying "ὅπου γὰρ τέλειος ἀνθρώπινος ἐκεῖ γὰρ ἁμαρτία" Vide also Lib: II, § 6, &c.
(20) Vide Rufinus [Eccl. Hist. Lib. II, cap. 20]; Nicephorus [Eccl. Hist. Lib. XVIII, cap. 51]; Theodoret [Eccl. Hist. Lib. V, cap. 3]; St. Gregory Nazianzen [1st Epist. to Cledonius, §§ 4 and 6]; St. Vincent of Lerins [Commin. cap. XII, § 14], &c.
(21) E. g. vide St. Athanasius [Contra Apoll. Lib. I, § 13 et seq.; and Lib. II, § 14 et seq.]; Theodoret [Exp. Pslm. XV, 10]; &c.

trine of the Person of Christ. This heresy—Nestorianism—stated that the Incarnation of our Lord was, in fact, but a mere "possession," or inspiration, by which the Logos dwelt *in* the man Jesus, Whom He there assumed. True, this "possession" of Jesus did not merely begin at His baptism (as Cerinthus had taught), but was from the moment of His conception; neither, again, did it cease at His crucifixion (as Cerinthus had also taught), but, on the contrary, continued then, as it will continue for evermore. Nevertheless it was, after all, but a mere "possession"—He was but "Θεοφόρος,"—and there were in Him two separable persons — the man Jesus, and the Logos; — so that the blessed Virgin, His mother, was but "Χριστοτόκος," not "Θεοτόκος,"[22] as the Church had said.

The fallacy of this most dangerous heresy is plainly evident. If, in the first place, such a theory were true, then, logically, there could be no real meaning to, or place for, either the Atonement wrought on Calvary, or the Sacramental system of the Church derived from that Atonement. For, obviously, under this supposition, the Inspiring Logos on the one hand, did not, and could not have suffered, died, and risen again; nor, on the other hand, could the passion, death, and resurrection of the man Jesus have had much more efficacy or benefit than that of any other Holy man. And yet further; if the Logos and the man Jesus were separable Persons, even if it be only in thought, then they evidently could have been divided; and, in fact, *were so divided* at the death, and burial of our Lord; so that at that time (under this supposition) the Incarnation, manifestly, must, for a season at least, have *ceased to be!* It is hard to see, if the Nestorian theory of our Lord's Person be the true one, how these conclusions can well be denied.

But even further: as I have already pointed out (pp. 14, 15), such mere "possession" would not, and could not, in any true sense of the word, constitute an "Incarnation" at all; for this, as I have stated, implies, not merely being *in* a man, but *being* a man; I will recur to this fact, and more fully elucidate it, when I treat of our Lord as the Primal Man.

And finally; if this Nestorian theory were true, and the man Jesus merely "joined to," and "inspired by" the Indwelling Logos, then we might well ask how such "possession" would greatly differ from the various examples of "Inspiration" already given (pp. 13-14). Surely, in such a case, Christianity, with all its vast superstructure of faith, and of doctrine, would be mistakenly founded upon a very ordinary event indeed—upon an event, in short, that is, in some degree, paralleled in the heart of every man!

So much then for Nestorianism: but turning now to the next heresy in order, namely the Eutychian, we find that the pendu-

---

(22) Which term, I need scarcely say, should, strictly, be translated "the God Bearer" [from "τίκτω"], or "Deipara," rather than "the mother of God;" this latter phrase being open to heretical misconstructions.

lum has swung the other way, and we are presented with a theory that is but little removed from the true and orthodox Faith. Thus Eutychianism said that while our Lord's human body, and human mind were real entities, and had a genuine existence, yet the powers of the latter of these—i. e. His human mind—were so "swallowed up," and overwhelmed by His Godhead as to be practically without operation. He could, then, "hunger;" but He could not be "ignorant:" for the "self-emptying"—the "κένωσις"—mentioned by St. Paul (Philip ii, 5–9), applied only to His body, and not to His human mind; inasmuch as this latter was "swallowed up in His Godhead, as is a drop of honey in the ocean."[23]

Now this question of the "Kenosis" is certainly a most difficult one, and its full treatment must be reserved to its proper sequence (vide chap. v): but yet an obvious objection to this Eutychian theory, and one that can be advanced here, is that it plainly lies open, nearly as much as Apollinarianism, to the charge of Doketic unreality. He Who freely assumed our perfect humanity, would surely not proceed to thus swamp and nullify one chief element in that humanity, namely its rational mind. Nay! inasmuch as that human mind, like all other finite reasons, must derive its very existence from His inspirational "light" (vide note 1, and pp. 42 and 43, &c.), He can hardly be thought to be so swamping and nullifying its action, at the same instant that He is giving it both its very being and guidance.

Although, then, some[24] have felt themselves forced to adopt this theory, or at least a modified form of it, out of a feeling of reverence for our Lord, yet such a course, is, I am sure, both unnecessary and wrong. For while, on the one hand, it introduces into our faith concerning our Lord's Incarnation the deadly virus of unreality, on the other hand, all reverent solicitude for the honor of our Lord is, as I hope to show, abundantly satisfied by the Catholic doctrine of His Person.

But from Eutychianism was developed the much more serious errors of Monophysitism, a somewhat broad term, covering a number of more or less variant sects. Their doctrine, as a whole, was a development on ultra-Eutychian lines, for they taught that the humanity was, not merely "swallowed up" and rendered inoperative, but actually *transfused into* the Godhead— Deified—in some inconceivable way.

To this Catholics replied that such a "transfusion" as this of the finite into the Infinite—the manhood becoming the God-

---

(23) This was the chosen simile of the Eutychians; see the "Eranistes, or Polymorphous" [Dialogue II, on "the Unconfused"] written by Theodoret against them. Yet St. Gregory of Nyssa [Adv. Apoll. § 42] used the same simile in exposition of the orthodox faith! This, of course, was before the heretical bearings of the analogy were clearly seen; yet it was, surely, always a dangerous and misleading simile to adopt.

(24) E. g. many of the "Schoolmen" [vide note 63 and p. 39]; who certainly, in their apparent predication of *Omniscience* to the *human* mind of our Lord came perilously near Eutychianism.

head—was utterly and entirely inconceivable; and in addition, if it were true, the result would be no true "Incarnation" at all; but rather a "third confused something," that would be neither God, nor man.

This Monophysite theory was revived in an even exaggerated form by the Lutherans of the Reformation period; for although their theology at first was strongly Nestorian in tendency,[25] yet they were ultimately led by their Eucharistic theory, first into Adoptionism; and thence into ultra-Monophysite thought; predicating, by their peculiar interpretation of the "communicatio idiomatum," all the qualities of the Godhead, even the Omnipresence, to the finite humanity of our Lord.

But it was reserved for the present age to give expression to an opposite, and if possible, even more absurd form of Monophysitism, namely the transfusion of the Divine into the human! The theory that the Infinite Logos "depotentiated" Himself, and entirely forsaking both the Unity of the Trinity, and the Universe that He upheld, became an utterly unconscious embryo; and passing through an ignorant, fallible, and peccable boyhood, to a manhood in which He was but dimly conscious of Himself, finally only attained, or rather recovered, the complete self consciousness of His Godhead by years of patient experience, this monstrous theory, I say, first[26] definitely broached by Zinzendorf, has been gravely advocated by Gess,[27] Godet,[28] and others of the Neo-Lutheran school, as the correct exposition of the "Kenosis" preached by St. Paul!!

Now, as I have already stated, in my treatment of Eutychianism, the full consideration of the very difficult question of the "Kenosis" must be reserved until its proper sequence; I will therefore merely say here that such a heresy as the above not only falls, like its more Christian analogue—Monophysitism proper,—into the grave philosophical absurdity of confounding the finite and the Infinite—the human and the Divine,—but it also, in an even blasphemous manner, makes the Absolute, for a season, even inferior to man!

Returning to the more sober heresies of the Church, we may note Monothelitism, an attempted compromise between the more moderate section of the Monophysites, and the Eastern Catholic Church. This theory stated that while our Lord, in His Incarnation, had doubtless the orthodox "*Two Natures*,"

---

(25) Inasmuch as their reproduction of, and strenuous insistence upon, the Gnostic theory of the total evilness of man, *as man*—all his *virtues*, even, being nothing more than additional sins,—would logically have led them, had they followed it out, into either a *Nestorian* view of our Lord's Incarnation [as was, in fact, at first Luther's own view; although later modified, as stated in the text, into an Adoptionistic theory: vide note 29]; or else into such an absurd and blasphemous theory as was actually put forth later by Gess, &c.; namely that the Infinite "depotentiated" Himself, and became a *sinful man!*

(26) Although we find it, previously, among the incoherent heresies of the various Anabaptist sects; and traces of it, again, occur among the Gnostics; for it was, apparently, substantially professed by Beron of the Valentinian school. [Vide St. Hippolytus. "Contra Beronem et Helicem."]

(27) Vide his "Die Lehre von der Person Christi."

(28) Vide his "Com: on the Gospel of St John."

yet nevertheless His *Will* was only *One;* and furthermore, that that Will belonged solely to His Divine Nature, His humanity being, in short, totally destitute of this faculty.

But, as the Catholics naturally replied, this not only injured our Lord's true humanity (for a human nature that lacked a will would be, at the least, very imperfect; even if it were not utterly inconceivable), but also it practically re-introduced an Apollinarian denial to our Lord of any real humanity, other than His mere physical existence.

But the full consideration of this heresy must be reserved until we treat of the "two wills" of our Lord (vide pp. 45 and 46); suffice it now to say that it was heretical, more in its deductions, than in its statements; and as I will show in its analysis, was but little removed from the true and orthodox Faith.

The last heresy that concerns us is that strange one of early Spain, known to theologians as the "Adoptionist" heresy. The accounts given of its character are extremely difficult to unravel; but it would seem that it started from a Nestorian basis, and reached Monophysitic conclusions.[29] Thus its advocates predicated in our Lord, primarily, *Two Persons*—the man Jesus, and the "Word,"—as did Nestorius; but the man Jesus was thought to have been gradually "assumed" by, or transfused into the "Word;" until at our Lord's Resurrection His Nature was but a Monophysitic *One*.[30] Hence they were willing both to anathematise Nestorius, whose "Two Persons," ever remained distinct, and to grant to the Blessed Virgin the title of "Θεοτόκος," in view of what her Son became.

Yet if such a doctrine were true, then the "Word" did *not* become "Incarnate by the Holy Ghost of the Virgin Mary;" but, on the contrary, was, during His life, *gradually becoming so* in some indefinable way. And furthermore; when this "gradual Incarnation" had been completed, not only would we have the incomprehensible "third something" of the Monophysites, that was neither God nor man; but we would also have to predicate the additional absurdity of a gradual annihilation and disappearance of the "Ego" of a man!

Such, then, are the various heretical theories concerning the Incarnation of our Lord; and in contradistinction to them all we have the doctrine of the Church, as laid down at the Council

---

(29) A similar fusion of these two heresies seems to have been previously held by some of the later and minor Monophysite sects; and hence very probably, its origin in Gothic Spain; being introduced there, from Egypt, by some of these heretics, following in the wake of the invading Moors.

It is, certainly, very Eastern in its subtlety, and unlike what Western thought would produce; and as such, indeed, it sorely puzzled the comprehension of the blunt Goths and Franks, who condemned it at the Councils of Frankfort, Aix la Chapelle, &c. And furthermore; it seems, to me, to be the legitimate conclusion to which Monophysite thought, at its ultimate analysis, must arrive. So that everything, in fact, both in its history, and its character, points to its primary origin in the East.

We may notice, too, in this connection, that "Adoptionism" was similarly embraced by Luther, as the logical transition from his earlier Nestorianism, to his later Monophysitism [vide Dorner " Person of Christ," part 2, vol. 2, sect. 1]; and as such, again, it has been the teaching of various Lutheran theologians; and, notably, of Dorner himself [vide part 2, vol. 3, pp. 250 et seq.]

(30) Vide Lib: II, 16, of the treatise of Felix, the Spanish originator of the heresy.

of Chalcedon, namely that while there were, and are in our Lord *Two distinct Natures*—the Divine, and the human,—yet their union is *"hypostatic"*[31] and of the closest possible character, so that He is but *One Person*—"for as the reasonable soul and flesh is *one man*, so God and man is *One Christ.*"[32]

It was not, then, by taking a man *unto* Him that He became Incarnate, as Nestorius, and the Adoptionists said; nor was it, again, by assuming, in any degree, the *illusionary appearance* of a man, as the "Doketic" heresy, and, in a lesser degree, Apollinarianism taught; nor, yet again, by either *blending* Himself with, or *changing* Himself into a man, as the various Monophysite heresies imagined. But it was, so to speak, by *creating a manhood around Him;* a manhood that had no conceivable existence apart from Him: and yet also one that was real and true, could hunger and thirst, endure anguish and temptation; and in short, as I hope to show, feel all the limitations of a natural human existence.

Thus if we may picture to ourselves man as a three fold being—Spiritual "Ego," mental life, and bodily life creating a body—then we can say that, in our Lord, the Logos was His "Ego;" and that His mental and bodily lives were real and genuine human ones, having for their Creative and Sustaining "Ego" the Divine Logos of God.

And, furthermore, even as it is true that in man the intellect, and the bodily life exist, and can only exist as "emanations" (so to speak) of the individual and hypostatic "Ego"; so, too, in Christ the human intellect, and the human bodily life could have, and did have, no possible existence apart from Him, either before He "assumed" them, or subsequent to that event.[33]

This is a most important point, for, as it will be noticed, it is precisely here that Nestorianism, on the one hand, and Monophysitism, with its various affiliations (i. e. Apollinarianism, Eutychianism, and Adoptionism), on the other, went so widely astray;[34] for they all made the primary mistake of conceiving of

---
(31) Vide the note. at the end of this treatise. on "the **Hypostatic Union in Christ.**"
(32) Compare Eph: ii, 15. "For to make in Himself of *twain, one* new man, &c."
(33) Vide the Essay on "Spirit and Matter."
(34) Vide St. Leo (Epist: xxviii "to Flavian." i. e. the "Tome." cap. 4; and again Epist: xxxv, "to Julian, bishop of Cos." cap. 3]; in which latter passage he says: "In eo **vero** quod Eutyches in episcopali judicio ausus **est dicere** 'ante Incarnationem duas in Christo fuisse naturas, post Incarnationem **autem** unam.'" * * * "Arbitror enim talia loquentem hoc habere persuasum, quod anima quam Salvator assumpsit prius in coelis sit **commorata** quam de Maria Virgine nasceretur, eamque sibi Verbum in utero copularet Sed hoc Catholicae mentes auresque non tolerant: quia nihil **secum** Dominus de coelo **veniens nostrae** conditionis exhibuit; nec animam enim **quae** anterior exstitisset, nec **carnem** quae non materni corporis esset accepit. Natura **quippe** nostra non sic assumpta est, ut prius creata, post assumeretur; *sed ut ipsa assumptione crearetur.* Unde quod in Origine merito damnatum est qui animarum **antequam** corporibus insererentur, non solum vitam, sed ut diversas, fuisse asseruit **actiones necesse est ut etiam in** isto nisi maluerit sententiam abdicare plectatur.'" Vide also St. John Damascene [De Fide Orth: Lib: iv, cap. 2; and Lib: iv, cap. 6;] St. Gregory Nazianzen [Orat: 36;] &c.

In fact, this was the source of error in *all* the **Christological heresies**, with the exception of Gnosticism, and its daughter Arianism; which sprang rather from an even more radical error, namely Dualism. But perhaps, analysing still deeper, Dualistic principles were the "fors et origo mali" in *every one* of these heresies; for their common initial mistake, noted above, of making the Incarnation a *combination* or *junc-*

our Lord's humanity as existing *previous* to the Incarnation, and therefore apart from Him; instead of regarding it, like the Catholics did, as *created by that Incarnation*.[35] The insoluble problem, therefore, that they set before themselves, was to Incarnate the Logos in a *separate* humanity; and that by making the Incarnation either a mere "possession" of the pre-existing humanity; or else an "absorption" or "transfusion" of that humanity into the overpowering Divinity.

But the true and Catholic faith is, I repeat, that the Humanity of our Lord had, and can have, no possible existence, either previous to, or apart from Him, Who was, and is, Its Hypostatic "Reality" and "Ego." This is what theologians mean when they speak of the Human Nature of our Lord as being an "impersonal personality;" and it is also the special point of distinction in saying that He assumed, "not *man*, but *humanity*."[36]

But yet, on the other hand, it was not, by any means, a mere "abstract humanity" that He assumed; for such an abstraction is purely notional to our minds, and is without any actual existence; but it was real and personal humanity, genuine and individual, given to Him, and Him alone, by her who conceived Him in her womb, and became thus the earthly "mother of her Lord."[37]

It follows, then, that the Incarnation, having once taken place, can never be undone; there can never be an "Excarnation;" but the Godhead, and the manhood are there joined together, never to be divided. And even when our Lord died upon the Cross, and His Human body was thereby parted from His human bodily life and intellect—the one to lie in the sepulcher, and the other (mind, and vital life) to descend to the "Hell" of the dead,—even then, I say, the "Hypostatic Union" was not impaired; for the Omnipresent Logos was with that lifeless body in the grave, as He was with His human Soul in "Hell;" being thus, during those three days, "locally manifest" in those two places.[38]

---

ture, in various ways, between God and a *pre-existent* man [or "humanity," as the case might be] came [as St. Leo points out, in the case of Origen] from their primary false conception of man's body [or "manhood"] as a sack, or cage, *into* which the "spirit" is put at birth; instead of rightly regarding it as the creation, and expression of the phenomenal relations, of that "spirit"—that "hypostatic Ego" [Vide the Essay on "Spirit and Matter."] And this erroneous anthropology came, in turn, from a Dualistic opposition between "Spirit" and "Matter."

(35) Vide St. Leo; quoted in the preceding note.
(36) Vide St. Augustine [De Fide; ad Petr: cap. 17;] St. Cyril Alex: [De Incar: Dom: cap. 32;] Peter Lombard [Liber Sent: Book iii, dist. 5, qq. 1 and 4;] St. Thomas Aquinas [Sum: Theo: Pars. iii, Q. iv, art. 2.] "Utrum Filius Dei assumpserit personam?" denied; &c.
(37) Vide St. John Damascene. [De Fide Orth: Lib: iii, cap. 11;] Peter Lombard [Liber Sent: Book iii, dist. 5, q. 5;] St. Thomas Aquinas [Sum: Theo: Pars. iii, Q. iv, art. 4;] &c. See also pp. 29 and 30, on the necessity, in relation to a real Incarnation, of a human conception and birth.
(38) Vide St. Thomas Aquinas [Sum: Theo: Pars iii, Q. L, art. 2.] "Utrum in morte Christi fuerit separata Divinitas a carne?" denied: so too Peter Lombard [Liber Sent: Book iii, dist. 21, qq. 1 and 2.] And St. Thomas Aquinas again [Q. idem, art. 3.] "Utrum in morte Christi fuerit facta separatio Divinitatis ab anima?" denied. See also p. 65 and note 110 on the "descent into Hell."

CHAPTER IV.

THE Logos, then, perfectly assumed our nature—mental and bodily,—joining it to Himself in One Inseparable Person; and He was able to do this—to be this "Ego" of a man, with a human intellect begotten of, and a human bodily life proceeding from that "Ego"—because, and only because He was the "Primal Adam"—the "Adam Quadmon" of the Cabbalists—in whose "Image" man had first been made.

It has, therefore, ever been taught, since the theology of the Incarnation was first clearly formulated, that our Lord could not have become Incarnate in a beast, or a plant, or even in an angel, as He did in man.

He could not, in the first place, have been so Incarnate in an animal, or a plant; and that because such beings lack the intellectual ability to know God; and are, therefore, manifestly incapable of being the media for an Incarnation of the "Word." While angels, on the other hand, although certainly able to know God, are yet also unable to receive Him, owing to their lack of such a common, corporate, and generic nature as could be assumed; arising from their want of the power of self propagation; and their consequent purely separate and underived individualities. While our Lord, then, might certainly have come *into* an angelic individual, and so possessed and inspired him in a Nestorian way (and this, as I have already shown, would have been no true "Incarnation"); yet He, obviously, could not have come into, and then absorbed, or annihilated that individuality, in an Adoptionist fashion; for this would be, not the "assumption" of an angelic nature, but simply the *destruction* of one; nor, again, could He have changed Himself into an angel; for this would involve the philosophical absurdity of a Monophysitic change of natures.

Our, Lord, then, I repeat, could not have become Incarnate in a plant, or a beast, whose generic nature would not be suitable; nor even in an angel, whose being lacks such a corporate and generic nature as might be assumed; but could only so tabernacle in man—a being who possesses a corporate nature kindred to His own, and originally made, in fact, in His likeness." Any other nature, then, than this He could, no doubt, have *possessed*, could have *inspired*, could have been (so to speak) a *Nestorian Christ;*

---

(39) Vide Peter Lombard [Liber Sent: Book iii, dist. 2, q. 1;] and St. Thomas Aquinas [Sum: Theo: Pars iii. Q. iv, art. 1;] who also divides the congruity for the Incarnation into a "congruity of dignity," and a "congruity of need;" and says that while animals, as non-intellectual, lack the former, angels, as unfallen, lack the latter. Yet see my remarks on pp. 71, 72 as to the non-essentiality of the "fall" to the Incarnation. And yet again; under the supposition of Aquinas, would not the *fallen angels* have an even greater "congruity," both of "dignity," and of "need," than man?

but He could not have *been it;* and this, as has been already noted, is what "Incarnation" really means.

And this fact of the Logos being the "Primal Adam"—the Archetypal Man—gives us the key to many obscurities. In the first place it shows us, as I have just explained, how God could become really a man; and not, on the one hand, be merely in a man, as Nestorius taught; nor yet, on the other hand, be only such an imitation man, as Doketism falsely imagined.

It again allows us, I think, to perceive, at least in some degree, the grand purpose of God in the Incarnation of His Son. This, apparently, was primarily to unify man with Him—the "image" with its Maker;—and only incidentally, as it were, to atone by suffering for the sins of man. I will touch upon this point again before I close.

And, finally, it gives us the plain reason why the Son or Logos of God, rather than the Father, or the Holy Spirit, became Incarnate in man. This seems to me perfectly simple, if we will but realize the following facts. In the first place, the Logos, as the Logos—the Word and Wisdom of God,—is the High Priest and Mediator to all Creation: from the Unknown, and Unknowable "Ἀρχή" of the Godhead—the "Father"—is Eternally Begotten the Plenary Essence of the "Son," Who is the "Express Image" of His Person—the Mediator and Revealer of His Will: — and from that "Ἀρχή," again, of the Father, through the Plenary Essence of the Son, Eternally Proceedeth that Holy Spirit, Who is the Lord and Giver of Life. If, then, in short, we may but name the Father "the Primal Cause," the Son "the Formal Cause," and the Holy Spirit "the Efficient Cause" of Creation, we may possibly gain a clearer conception both of the inter-relations of the Three Blessed Persons in the Trinity, and also of the reason for the special Incarnation of One of those Persons—namely the "Formal Cause" and "Wisdom"—in man; inasmuch as he had been made in that "Wisdom's" likeness.

And man was made in this "likeness" because it was most fitting and indeed necessary, that he—an intelligent, moral, and spiritual being, created (as we believe) to love and serve his God—should be, to his finite capacity, a mirror and representative of the Divine Logos of God.

True it is that, in some sense, every created being, and Creation itself as a whole, must be, to a greater or less degree, an "image" and reflection of the Logos; and that because He is, as I have said, the "Creative and Formal Cause;" this thought I have already hinted at in the beginning of this treatise (pp. 1, 2) when speaking of the "λόγοι" in Nature, and the testimony they bear to Him.

And similarly, to draw out an analogy, may we not also say that the creations of man—his books, his mechanism, or his buildings—all bear the impress of their author; and reflect, in their degree, his personality and "image." Reflect, I say, in their degree; for, manifestly, the higher and more intellectual our creation is in its character, the more of our individuality do we give to it; and consequently, the more perfectly, also, will it mirror us forth. Thus, for example, a biographical novel, or a philosophical theory will, evidently, bear far more of our "image" than any mechanism we may invent; and this latter, again, witness far more concerning us than the house or monument we may build.

Carrying on the analogy, then, may we not surely say that while all things in the Cosmos must, and do reflect the Logos; yet this reflection is more or less perfect according to their respective rank in the scale of being;[40] or in other words, according as they partake more or less of an intellectual, moral, and spiritual character; and finally, that it is in man, and man alone, who, as I have already remarked, was created especially to know and love Him, that we must look for such an especial reflection, as will warrant us in speaking of him as being, more peculiarly, in the "image" of that Logos of God.

And in fact it is only because there is this likeness and "image" that God can, in any degree, be known to man; for were there no common predicates between man and his God,—no likeness by which (as is said on pp. 9 and 10) God can be known anthropometrically—then there would, manifestly, be no relation—no connotation—between ourselves and our Maker; and He would therefore be absolutely and entirely unknowable.

But this necessary likeness being allowed, it follows then, as I have shown, that the Logos, and the Logos alone, could be Incarnate; and that both by reason of His inherent Priesthood, and of His Archetypal relation to man.[41]

True it is that in a sense, it was not the Logos alone Who was manifest in Christ; but both the Father and the Holy Spirit were working through that humanity, by reason of the necessary circumincession (περιχώρησις) and co-working of the Persons of the Blessed Trinity among Themselves.[42] Nevertheless the Father, and the Holy Spirit were not, properly speaking, *Incarnate*—were not *man;*—but were only, so to speak, Nestorian "possessions," or *in* the man; and It was the Logos, and the Logos *alone*, Who was the "Son of Man"—Who became, in other words, actually Incarnate, in any true sense of the term.

This truth, then, of the Logos like "image" of man is the key that explains much in the Incarnation; showing how, in reality,

---
(40) And, in fact, determines that **rank**.
(41) Vide St. Thomas Aquinas [" Sum: Theo:" Pars iii Q iii. art. 8;] St. John Damascene ["De Fide Orth:" Lib iv, cap. 4;] St. Bernard ["Sermo de Adventu." 1;] Richard de St. Victor ["Lib: de Verbo Incar:" cap. 8 et seq.;] St. Athanasius ["De Incar: Verbi Dei," §§ 1-5; and "Four Discourses against the Arians," 2nd disc: cap. 62 et seq. on "πρωτότοκος;"] St. Augustine [Tract: in Joan: li. 2;] St. Clemens Alex: ["Strom:" Lib: v, cap. 14; "Paed:" Lib: i. cap. 3] &c. Vide also notes 51 and 52.
(42) Vide St. Augustine ["De Trinitate," Lib: ii. cap. v. 9 and "De Fide; ad Petr:" cap. 2;] Peter Lombard [Liber Sent: Book iii, dist: 1, q. 3.] &c.

God became Man; why He became Man; and finally, why it was the Logos Who thus became Man; as it is, again, the key to the Christian doctrine of sin and redemption;[43] yet it is also a truth that is liable, on the other hand, to be fearfully misapprehended.

For men have taken this likeness, and pressed it far beyond anthropometric, to even anthropomorphic limits; and have plainly said that humanity and Divinity are, at the bottom, the same—that the ultimate terms of the one, are also the ultimate terms of the other;—and even that humanity raised to its highest powers becomes Divinity!

True it is, as I have already stated, that we can only know God in a manlike way—can only predicate Him in terms of our highest perfections (such as "personality," "thought," "volition," and "holiness"); which, in truth, He must, at least, possess, seeing that He is the Creator, and Sustainer of these perfections in us.—But by what right, or what law of thought, can we possibly *limit* the Absolute to these qualities, and say that *we* are the final measure of all things—the *Absolute* in fact, — so that "humanity raised to its highest powers—its most perfect expression—becomes Divinity!" Such language is, evidently, rankly anthropomorphic, and is worse than absurd; for if it has any meaning at all, it can only imply a heathen "apotheosis."

Humanity, then, and Divinity are *not* fundamentally the same;[44] and still less does humanity ever become Divinity; nevertheless the human nature that the Logos assumed was, I repeat, a nature akin to His own, inasmuch as it had been created in His "image." Thus as Canon Mason in his "Faith of the Gospel" (p. 150) has finely said, "the natures of God and man are not contradictory to each other, as life and death are, or holiness and

---

(43) Vide the Essay on "**the Essential Nature of Sin.**"
(44) Vide St. John Damascene [De Fide Orth: Lib: iii, cap. 2;] and St. Thomas Aquinas [Sum: Theo: Pars iii, Q. xvi, art. 7;] who both deny that man was *Deified* by the Incarnation; and St. Thomas [Q. idem, art. 5.] further denies that the same things can be predicated of humanity and Divinity

And this consideration, as I may here remark, evidently entirely cuts away any such attempted explanation of our Lord's Divinity, as that put forward, in the early history of the Church, by Artemon, and Paul of Samosata; namely, that our Lord was originally nothing more than a man; but that He attained Divinity as a reward for His unusual virtue.

Such an idea is so utterly absurd, contradicting, as it does, the most elementary theological and philosophical axioms, that it needs no refutation here; it is, in short, only explicable as the importation of the thoroughly heathen conception of an "apotheosis"—the promotion of a dead hero to a "Divinity" that differed widely from the Christian and Theistic meaning of the word.

And yet, strange to say, this teaching, at least in its **main** features, has been reproduced, of late years, by Ritschl, and his school in Germany; but with this portentous exception: to Paul of Samosata, and his followers, both the Godhead, and our Blessed Lord, were objectively real and true; their heresy being simply, as I have stated, the heathen absurdity of an "apotheosis;" but to Ritschl, and his disciples, both God, and Christ are mere humanly projected ideals; and the "Divinity" that Christ attained, only our subjective appreciation of Him as our religious Hero! Whether Jesus of Nazareth really performed certain things—whether, in fact, He ever really existed,— does not matter, they say, in the slightest degree; inasmuch as His name is merely a convenient synonymn to us for our humanistic ideal!!

This is, evidently, Idealism run mad; and is far worse than a sincere and open Atheism; for it chooses, as its watchword, *conscious unreality and lies*. It is, then, rather a heresy against primary truth, and religious honesty, than a strictly *Christological* error; and has, therefore, with the heresies of Paul of Samosata, and of Ebionism, been omitted from consideration in my text.

sin. To conceive of a union between two such mutually exclusive terms as those is impossible; but not between God and man." " And again (p. 173), "in the unity of His Person all contradiction was reconciled; and the same things which became Him as Son of God, became Him as Son of man" * * * "This double aspect of each and all of our Lord's works must never be forgotten. He was not, by one series of acts, showing Himself as Son of God, and by another as Son of Man. There was in him no alternation between two parts which were to be played. He was continuously and harmoniously both. Thus we may, for clearness of study, contemplate His whole life and death, first as the manifestation of God to man, and secondly as the representation of man to God."

Our Lord, then, was the "Primal Adam;" and as such was truly Incarnate in man; being, at one and the same time, both Very and True God, and Very and True Man—the Logos "Ego," and the human mind and life;—and this fact throws a flood of light upon the meaning of, and necessity for, His Virgin Birth.

Had He been merely a Nestorian Christ—a man "indwelt by God," — and His mother only "Χριστοτόκος," not "Θεοτόκος" as well, then, humanly speaking, there would have been no particular necessity for, or meaning in, such an unprecedented miracle. For if merely a holy and obedient being had been required for the Logos to dwell *in*, then surely it would have been amply sufficient for a sanctified *father* to have been provided, as a sanctified *mother* was, in the person of the Holy Maid. But for a *Logos-ensouled humanity — not man,* — such as our Lord assumed, any earthly father would, manifestly, be inconceivable.

And furthermore, as I may point out, it was only by reason of this Virgin Birth that He was able to be, not a mere Palestinian Jew of the first century, with certain inherited family peculiarities and "atavisms," but on the contrary, the Archetypal Representative of *all* humanity—the Very "Son of *Man.*" In fact we may even say that if such a necessary truth as the Virgin Birth of our Lord had not been recorded in the Gospels, it would have been a serious difficulty; and one not to be easily reconciled with the other known facts of His Person.

But considering this Virgin Birth from another aspect, it is again evident that this motherhood of Mary was also an essential: as otherwise He would not have assumed a real humanity.

Thus some have asked the question why our Lord did not create and assume a manhood already matured: and so have escaped the fancied ignominy of being a human embryo, and of undergoing a human birth.

---

(45) Compare also St John Damascene [De Fide Orth: Lib: iii, cap. 2.] "*Ὧν γὰρ φύσει τέλειος Θεός, γέγονε φύσει τέλειος ἄνθρωπος ὁ 'αυτός ὂν τραπεὶς τὴν φύσιν οὐδὲ φαντάσας τὴν οἰκονομίαν.*" κ. τ. λ.; and St. Leo uses similar language [Sermo lxii. cap. 2; and Epist: cxxiv. § 5, "to the monks of Palestine."] "Utraque essentia communes habent actiones;" &c.

In answer to this we may say that such a question not only implies a Manichaean, and unchristian depreciation of "matter," and the "flesh," but also overlooks the all important fact that our Lord, as Very Man, must needs have undergone all the various phases of our natural life—our prenatal existence, our birth, and our childhood, no less than our manhood, and death;—for thus, and only thus, was He fully identified with us, and so enabled to accomplish His redemptive work.

But going even deeper than this, we may say that it was by such a human conception and birth, and by it alone, that our Lord was able to be, not merely a *full* man, but a *true man at all*. In other words, if He had so directly created His humanity, and not naturally assumed it from the Virgin, He could hardly have been of one race with ourselves; but would, on the contrary, have been, at the most, merely a Being with a human aspect. For, referring back to what I have said of the impossibility of His being Incarnate in an angel, owing to the lack of such a common angelic nature as could be assumed (p. 25), we may similarly say that it was only by His thus partaking, by a natural human birth from a woman, in this common human nature of ours, that He was able, as I have said, to be a true man at all.

We believe, then, both by Catholic logic, and by the plain testimony of the Gospels, that the Creative Spirit formed in the womb of the Holy Virgin the living primal germ of the humanity that was to be the earthly tabernacle of the Incarnate Son; a tabernacle that was never, from its beginnings, separate from Him; and which drew aliment from, and grew to natal maturity in, the protective and sustaining womb of her who was the "mother of her Lord."

And this miraculous conception, although certainly unprecedented, is not (biologically speaking) by any means so impossible an occurrence as is often pretended. "Parthenogenesis" is actually the rule in the lower and primary forms of life;[46] and the contrary fact is as purely a specialised function as say the functions of the eye or the ear. *Human* "parthenogenesis," then, is no more "prima facie" impossible, than is human sight without an eye, a thing by no means inconceivable.[47] Given, then, as under the Christian hypothesis of the Virgin Birth, a human life germ, created by the Holy Spirit of God, and the subsequent growth and development of that life germ into a perfect human body would be a perfectly natural, and indeed necessary occurrence.

I may further point out that there also exists an unnoticed,

---

(46) Taking the word to mean, not merely the phenomenon of "alternate generation" [to which, in zoology, the term is generally restricted], but also that reproduction by "budding," which is the law of the primary cell; and which can, surely, be described in no other way

(47) For might not the "light" vibrations possibly be transferred, say by electricity, *directly* to the optic nerve, and thence to the brain, without being first imprinted on the retina?

and yet (in some respects) close parallel to this natural growth of an unusually planted life germ, in the recent developments of surgical "transplanting." In this operation a foreign bone, or piece of flesh is grafted into a living body, and thereupon proceeds to draw sustenance from, live in, and finally be assimilated to that body; this surely is, to all practical intents, a "non-natural birth" of the aforesaid bone, or piece of flesh.

If this be so, then the only non-natural feature of the Virgin Birth is this primary creation by the Holy Spirit of the life germ; and if Christ be the Incarnate Logos of God (and to this truth all the facts of His life and doctrine testify), then any other origin for His humanity would, manifestly, be utterly incompatible.

There is yet another point that ought not to be omitted in this connection, and that is the doctrine of the "$\alpha\epsilon\iota\pi\acute{\alpha}\rho\vartheta\epsilon\nu o\varsigma$," or "Ever Virginity" of Mary. This doctrine, although not directly mentioned in the New Testament, is yet most congruous to the facts there given; and is, moreover, part of the Universal and Catholic tradition of the Church;[48] having been never so much as called in question by any professedly orthodox, or even heterodox Christian (with the exception of the ignorant Helvidius,[49] the disciple of the Arian Auxentius), until the unhappy divisions of the last four centuries. Some of the Gnostics, it is true, and the Ebionites denied it; but in every instance (with the possible exception of Helvidius just mentioned) those who did so, denied also the Virgin Birth, and the Godhead itself; making Jesus only the human son of Joseph the carpenter; and thus put themselves outside the pale of even heretical Christianity.

And even now (apart from an unreasoning antipathy to it, because of its supposed Roman affiliations) the only arguments that are alleged against it are the mentions of our Lord's "brethren" in St. Matt., xii, 46, and St. John, ii, 12. But even aside from the proverbial looseness of the term "brethren" in the East, these were certainly not his full brothers; but were probably either His half brothers, or His cousins; and this because they were, from all indications, *older* than he; as indeed we know was the case with one of them, namely "James, the brother of the Lord."

Returning to the Miraculous Conception itself, we may say that the question which so exercised the minds of many during the Middle Ages, namely as to the specific channel through which this Creation was effected, and whether it were not through the ear, need not detain us now, inasmuch as it entirely overlooks the vital point in that Conception. It was *not* an introduction from without of a *pre-existent germ*,[50] through the ear or otherwise;

---

[48] E. g. vide St. Athanasius ["Ora': ii, contra Arian:" § 70; and "Com: in Pslm. lxxxiv," § 11; and "Com: in Luc:" § 26;] Decrees of the Council of Chalcedon [Evagrius. "Eccl: Hist." Lib:ii, cap 4, p 200;] &c

[49] Some of the Apollinarians and Eunomians are *said* to have also denied it, at least implicitly; but yet this is not absolutely certain; and in any case, even if they did so, it was only as reproducing Gnostic teaching.

[50] Which, in fact, would be only a modification of the "tanquam per canalem" theory of the Gnostics. [Vide p 17.]

but, on the contrary, it was a new creation—a prime vivification—"*in situ*" by the Omnipresent Lord and Giver of Life, concerning Whom any transmission through space is inconceivable.

And if it be further asked why the creation of this primal germ of our Lord's body should have been the work of the Third Person of the Godhead—the Holy Spirit,—rather than of the Second Person—the Logos—Who inhabited that body, and gave it constant being, we can only say that in thus speaking of the Holy Spirit as the *especial* Agent, we by no means exclude the simultaneous co-working of either the Logos, or the Father. The creation, in short, of that primal germ was the work of the Godhead, as such;[51] and if it is also spoken of as being especially the work of the Holy Spirit, the reason is probably to be found in His Personal Relation in the Divine Essence. Thus, if we revert to my conception of the Father as the "Primal Cause," the Son as the "Formal Cause," and the Holy Spirit as the "Efficient Cause" in creation (page 26), we can possibly see why the creation of the primal germ of our Lord's humanity was the especial work of Him Who is, in a supreme manner, the Efficient Underlying Reality—the Lord and Giver of Life and Being—to all the Creation, animate, or inanimate, of God.[52]

There is yet another question that might be asked, and that is why our Lord assumed a masculine nature, and not a feminine one? In answer to this we may say that, while He, obviously, must have chosen one of the two, there was much, both in His life and work, that rendered the masculine form the only one fit or suitable.

But going even deeper than this, is there not a further reason in the fact that while true masculinity can, and does include true femininity, yet the contrary is not the case; or in other words, did not our Lord, in assuming the masculine nature, assume with it, as the major and inclusive one, also the feminine; and would He not, on the other hand, have failed to so include masculinity, had He become a woman?

But whether this be true or not, at least we can say that there were in His character these two diverse species of humanity. For if His stern reproofs of hypocrisy, and His steadfast facing of death, were instances of His true masculinity, no less was His tactful care for the multitude in the wilderness (St. Matt., xv, 32;

---

(51) Vide Peter Lombard [Liber Sent: Book iii. dist. 1, q. 4; and dist. 4, qq 1 and 2; and dist. 5, q. 1.] which latter passage reads as follows. "Et cum tota Trinitas operata sit formationem suscepti hominis quoniam inseparabilia sunt opera Trinitatis, solus tamen Filius accepit hominem in singularitatem personae, non in Unitatem Divinae Naturae; id est, quod est proprium Filii, non quod commune est Trinitati." See also St. Augustine ["De Trin:" Lib: i, cap. 4 and 5;] and St. Thomas Aquinas, quoted in the note following.

(52) Vide St. Thomas Aquinas [Sum: Theo: Pars iii. Q. xxxii. art. 1.] "Conceptionem corporis Christi tota Trinitas est operata." * * * "Ad primum ergo dicendum, quod opus conceptionis commune quidam est toti Trinitati; secundum tamen modum aliquem attribuitur singulis Personis. Nam Patri attribuitur auctoritas respectu Personae Filii, qui per hujus modi conceptionem sibi assumpsit humanam naturam. Filio autem attribuitur ipsa carnis assumptio. Sed Spiritui Sancto attribuitur formatio corporis quod assumitur a Filio."

St. Mark, viii, 3) a plain manifestation of the feminine pole in His nature. Surely in this respect, as in all others, He was not merely a man alone, but the true Representative of humanity—the very "Son of Man."

There is yet another interesting point that ought not be overlooked, and that is what we may term the "*secretness*" of the Virgin Birth; for it seems to have been utterly unknown to the Jews of our Lord's time,[53] and even to His early disciples.[54] It was, in short, as St. Ignatius said,[55] one of "the three mysteries of shouting," (the other two being our Lord's Messiahship, and the Atoning character of His death) "which were wrought in silence by God."

And the reason for this "secretness" is not hard to see. In the first place, it would naturally be a matter that would be known only to Mary, and to her betrothed husband Joseph, and possibly also to a few of her relations; and as something that would be peculiarly liable to the cavillings and blasphemies of the ignorant and unbelieving, it would hardly be further spread.

But more than this; it was also something that could have no possible meaning apart from the Divinity of our Lord. Once acknowledge both His Godhead, and His Archetypal relation to mankind, and, as I have just shown, His Virgin Birth becomes a logical necessity. But let that Essential Nature be unknown to, or unbelieved by men, and at once the Birth is without meaning or congruity. The first step, therefore, was to reveal *Himself*; and then, and only then, would the various peculiarities of His Nature, and among these, especially His unique Birth, be both comprehensible, and explicable.

And furthermore, as I may here remark, this self-revelation of our Lord must needs have been, as it was, a gradual educationary process. Had He come in the "μορφή" of the Godhead (were such a thing possible), no doubt all could, and would have believed in Him; but coming, as He did, in the "μορφή" of man—in the "local limitations" of His Incarnation,—it was manifestly, difficult for men to see that this real and true man was, in verity, the Incarnate Logos of God. For the first thirty years, then, of His life, and until the commencement of His ministry, there would obviously, have been no suitable occasion for, or indeed meaning in, such a revelation; and even after His ministry opened, the process must have been a gradual one; and in fact it was not until the grand confession of St. Peter "Thou art the Christ, the Son of the Living God" (St. Matt., xvi, 16), that any, even of His nearest and dearest disciples, seemed to realise, in any degree, Who He really was; a realisation that was not perfected until after His Resurrection.

---

[53] Vide, for instance, their words "Is not this Jesus, the *son of Joseph?*" [St. John vi, 42; also St. Luke iv, 22; St. Matt: xiii, 55; St. Mark vi, 3.]
[54] Vide the words of St. Philip [St. John i, 45.]
[55] "Epistle to the Ephesians," § 19.

CHAPTER V

THE Infinite and Omnipresent Logos, then, having become Incarnate, and "made man," by the primal Will of the Father, and through the operation of the Creative Spirit, was thus *locally manifested* to His world; and furthermore, as I have said, also *locally limited* by reason of the medium of that manifestation, namely the humanity: this brings us to one of the main facts in that Incarnation; and one, moreover (as has been already remarked), that is often grieviously misapprehended and misapplied; namely what is known to theologians as the "Kenosis," or "self emptying" of the Son.

This is often expounded as if He therein laid aside, and abrogated the powers and attributes of His Godhead—as if, in short, He thereby practically annulled His Divinity.[56] Yet such a "conversion of the Godhead into flesh" as this implies is surely something that is utterly and entirely unthinkable. For the attributes of the Godhead—His Power, His Love, His Knowledge, His Justice—are certainly not separable, the one from the other; but are, accurately speaking, only distinguishable as convenient concepts to our minds, imaging forth to us various aspects of His Infinite and Indivisible Unity. He can, then, no more "lay aside," or relinquish His Knowledge, or His Power, than He can His Nature Itself.

And it is, if possible, even still more inconceivable that the Son *alone* should thus abrogate His Essential Nature in the Triune God, to the exclusion of the Father and the Holy Spirit.[57] This absurdity, which in fact (as I have already stated in note 12) is only even imaginable under a thoroughly *Trideistic* conception of the Trinity, I have, I think, fully exposed when introducing the doctrine of the "local manifestation."

And, in addition, we might ask, if indeed any further argument is required, if this "laying aside" by the Son of His Power, would not be also a "laying aside" of His ability to redeem? Such a "depotentiation" as this, in order that He might become Incarnate, would surely sacrifice the very reason itself for which that Incarnation was undertaken, namely to draw man to God, and incidentally to also redeem him from sin.

But while any abrogation, or annulling by the Logos of the Essential Powers of His Godhead—such as His necessary Infinite Wisdom, and Power—is utterly unthinkable and absurd, yet

---

(56) Which, as explained on p. 21 and in note 12 is the theory of the "Kenosis," advocated by Zinzendorf, Gess, Godet, and others!
(57) As is taught, not only by Zinzendorf, Gess, and Godet, but even by Ebrard, Thomasius, and in fact the majority of the Neo-Lutheran theologians!

the *local manifestation* that characterized His Incarnation, necessarily carried with it a *local limitation, by the medium of that manifestation, of the action of those Essential Powers*.[38]

For inasmuch as it was a *human* mind, and a *human* body that He assumed, and *through* which He worked, it is plainly evident that *strictly superhuman works could not be wrought through them*. The human organism—body, and mind—is, no doubt, capable of heroic deeds, and of great endurance; but it is certainly not possessed of infinite powers; and its capabilities, after all, are exceedingly finite and limited.

Thus, in the first place, the body, with its cosmos of nerves and of muscles, becomes rapidly weary; and in such a case, imperatively needs refreshment and rest; and it can, therefore, and indeed *must* suffer hunger, weariness, and pain. Our Lord, then, in assuming a body, necessarily assumed with it the natural conditions of that body; and it was, therefore, in no deceptive or Doketic fashion that He hungered and slept, and suffered bitter agony and pain.

But if the body of man is finite and passible, so also is the human intellect. It is true that the mind of man is, in its stupendous powers, the most Godlike thing with which we are acquainted. It is capable of such profound reasoning, it has made such sublime discoveries, it has given birth to such magnificent creations, that the temptation has ever been to bow down before it as our God. Yet we must never forget that it is, after all, by the very constitution of its being, finite; and therefore utterly incapable of Omniscience; and although we may fancy, in our pride of intellectuality, that its capabilities for reasoning and for knowledge are practically boundless, yet in every direction the limit is speedily reached, and impotence or madness bar our further way.

Inasmuch, then, as our Lord took a real and operative human mind (and this, as I have already shown, pp. 18-20, is essential to the reality of His Incarnation), He necessarily took with it its limitations, and ignorance. To deny this, and to insist that, in His "local manifestation" as the Christ, He was as Omniscient as He is in the Omnipresent Estate of the Logos, is not only to overlook the close and necessary interconnections there are between Omniscience and Omnipresence, but it is also to fall into the serious error of Eutyches, or even of the Monophysites; and thus to eviscerate the Incarnation of all real meaning. For if the humanity was "swallowed up in the Divinity," and rendered inoperative, and still more if it was even "transfused into the Divinity," and made One Nature, then for that reason, may we ask, was it assumed at all? For, as is shown on pp. 20 and 21,

---

(38) "Ἐν 'αυτῷ κατοικεῖ πᾶν τὸ πλήρωμα τῆς θεότητος σωματικῶς"
[Coloss: ii, 9.]

under either one of these suppositions, He was not, in any real sense, a true man; and we are thereby driven to assume either a practically Doketic view of His life and sufferings, and to think of them as merely a simulated deception; or else we must formulate our thoughts on strictly Monophysitic lines, and even absurdly predicate passibility to the Deity.

Either side of this dilemma is, manifestly, utterly untenable; and we are, therefore, forced to acknowledge the reality, and operation of our Lord's human mind, as we do that of His human body; frankly recognising the necessary finite limitations of the same. He Who is the Omniscient, Omnipotent, Omnipresent and Eternal Logos of God was, by His "local assumption" in time of, and "local manifestation" through, a finite nature that had been made in His own image, necessarily limited by that nature—only working with that body, and thinking with that brain, the works and thoughts that the said body and brain were able to perform and endure.

But even furthermore: our Lord assumed—created around Him—not only the intellectual faculties of the mind—its cold and colorless powers of reasoning,—but also those warmer, and more highly individualised emotional qualities—passions, affections, and sympathies — that are so inseparably part of the nature of man.

Thus we are plainly told that our Lord "wept" (St. John, xi, 35); "loved" (St. Mark, x, 21; St. John, xi, 5), "was moved with compassion" (St. Matt., ix, 36; St. Mark, vi, 34; viii, 2), and with "indignation" (St. Matt., xvii, 17), that He "groaned" (St. John, xi, 33), and finally, "began to be sorrowful, and very heavy" (St. Matt. xxvi, 37; St. Mark, xiv, 33; St. Luke, xxii, 44); all emotions that evidently belong, and belong only to our Lord's human emotional nature; for the Godhead, as the Absolute and Eternal, is manifestly Impassible and Unchangeable. It is entirely owing, I think, to the practical oversight of this emotional part of our Lord's humanity that so many of His recorded experiences, and especially His Awful Agony in the Garden, and on the Cross, are so often found entirely indecipherable and obscure; and I will therefore, in treating of that Agony and Crucifixion, recur to this emotional nature of our Lord; and unfold (as far as may be) its bearings upon those awful mysteries.

And finally: all these faculties, and elements of our Lord's real humanity were absolutely perfect; and that both in themselves, and in their several inter-relations and balance: in other words, there was in Him neither excess, nor defect in any part of His humanity; but He was, as the Archetypal man, the Perfect Representative of our race.

Our Lord, then, possessed a natural and passible human body, perfect in all its parts; and also a natural and passible human mind, perfect in all its faculties for both thought and emotion. And this leads us on to the subject of His *growth*, both in stature, and in knowledge.

This latter fact, namely the increase in knowledge, has been fiercely controverted by many, under the impression that such a "growth" would be derogatory to the dignity of the Incarnate Word: yet it is surely a fact that is as plainly taught us in Holy Scripture as is the corresponding "growth" in His Body (vide St. Luke, ii, 52). That He was an infant, and from that grew to man's estate, being subject, during the process, and in His subsequent life, to all the natural limitations of His body, and to its hunger, weariness, and pain, all this, I think, is freely accepted by every one who professes, in any degree, to follow the Gospel record.

And that His strictly analogous "growth" in knowledge, and the natural limitations of His human mind,[39] have not been as freely acknowledged, but have, on the contrary, been explained away, is due, I think, solely and entirely, to preconceived theories of an Eutychian character.

Yet surely we ought, in the first place, to fit our theories to the facts as given us, and not reverse the process; and secondly, such a suppression, or explaining away of facts, as Eutychianism, or semi-Eutychianism calls for, is, as I hope to show, not at all necessary under the true and Catholic theory of our Lord's Person. He, I repeat, the Omniscient, Omnipresent, Impassible and Eternal Logos, took, and locally limited Himself by, a finite and passible humanity—body, bodily life, and mind;—and in so doing necessarily subjected Himself to the laws governing that humanity—to the capacity for growth, the finite limitations, and the liability to suffer pain, incident to a real human body; to the similar capacity for growth, the finite limitations, and the liability to suffer anguish, incident to a real human mind;—and the finite limitations, the growth, and the pain are every whit as conceivable and necessary in one direction as the other. As He hungered, and was fed, so He came to know; as His body was racked with pain, so His soul was with anguish; and finally, as He grew from

---

(39) Thus we are told, not only that He "increased in wisdom and stature" [St. Luke ii, 52], but also that He "marvelled" [St. Matt: viii, 10; St. Mark vi, 6], and even came to know [St. Mark viii, 17; and xi, 13]. These are, evidently, the workings of a real and *finite* human mind; for in His Godhead, as the "All-Knowing," He manifestly cannot realise anything more intensely at one time, than another; and cannot, therefore, either "marvel," or "come to know."

And so, yet again, have we our Lord's own statement [St. Mark xiii, 32] that He, as the "Son," did not know the day of judgment. This, from the context [inasmuch as He is there classed with *finite* and *created* beings—i. e. angels and men]—is, most naturally, to be interpreted of His human manifestation, and its limitations; and thus indeed, it has, almost unanimously, been interpreted by the Fathers, and later Doctors: vide St Athanasius ["Contra Arian:" Lib: iii, cap. 37]; St. Ambrose ["On the Holy Spirit," Lib: ii. cap. 11, § 117; and "On the Christian Faith," Lib: v. cap. 4, § 191 et seq.]; St. Gregory Nazianzen ["Fourth Theo: Orat:" § 15]; St. Gregory the Great ["Epist: x, § 39]; St. Bernard [De Grad: Hum: cap. 3, §§ 10-11]; &c. In short, the *only* authority [so far as I am aware] who does not so explain this text, but refers it rather to the Essential Subordination of the Son, is St Basil [Epist: viii, § 17; and ccxxxvi]; and even he gives the ordinary interpretation as an alternative. And in furtherance of this exposition we may also note St. Matt: xxiv, 36; and especially Acts i, 7, spoken by our Lord after His resurrection.

a babe to man's estate, so His mind expanded in an equal degree—He "increased in wisdom and stature, and in favour with God and man."

To still further enforce this truth of the natural growth in knowledge we may point out that an infant's mind is manifestly incapable of conceiving, or even of containing, the thoughts of a mature man; a perfect babe, a perfect child, a perfect man, are all as different in their several capabilities and capacities for thought, as they are for action: would He, then, Who assumed a *perfect* humanity, during His infancy, conceive with that infant brain a man's thoughts—still less the thoughts of Infinitude;—or would He, in so doing, be a perfect human babe? Surely not! Catholic logic, equally with Holy Writ, assures us that the "growth" must have been as real in this respect as in the other; and that He Who assumed a perfect humanity, progressed naturally from childhood to youth, and from that to man's estate; being, in each succeeding age, a real and perfect human being, with the proper limitations, and powers of that age.[60]

His "growth," then,—in mind, as in body—was no mere Doketic "seeming," but was a genuine reality; and this is the true and vital "Kenosis" spoken of by St. Paul (Philip, ii, 6-8), in which He Who had been in the "$\mu o \rho \phi \acute{\eta}$"—the Divine Estate—of God, clung not to it, but locally took the "$\mu o \rho \phi \acute{\eta}$"—the human estate—of a man;[61] and "locally limiting" Himself by the necessary conditions of that manhood, humbled Himself, even unto the death of the Cross.

It was, in short, such a "self emptying"—such a "self limitation"—as was inseparable from a true Incarnation; but it was *not* as has already been stated (p. 34), such a "depotentiation" as would, in effect, have rendered that Incarnation powerless and useless.

A vital point, therefore, and one we must never forget, is as follows: although there was this "local limitation," yet nevertheless, *It was the Logos Who was thus manifesting Himself;* it

---

(60) Vide St. Thomas Aquinas [Sum: Theo: Pars iii, Q. xiii, art. 1.] "In mysterio Incarnationis ita facta est unio in persona, quod tamen remansit distinctio naturarum, utraque scilicet natura retinente id quod sibi est proprium" * * * "cum igitur anima Christi sit pars humanae naturae, impossibile est quod omnipotentiam habeat." And again, [Q. xii, art. 2.] "Utrum Christus in hac scientia profecerit?" affirmed. See also St. Athanasius ["Contra: Arian:" Lib: iv]; St. Basil [Epist: viii]; St. Gregory Nazianzen ["Fourth Theo: Orat." § 15]; St. Cyril Alex: ["Thes:" Lib: xxii]; St. Ambrose ["De Incar: Dom:" cap. 7]; St. Hilary ["De Trin" Lib: x, cap. 8, et seq.]; &c.

(61) Vide St. Augustine [Prosper. "Sent: ex Aug: delib:" 328] 'Reliquit Christus Patrem" * * * "non quia deseruit, et recessit a Patre: sed quia non in ea *forma* apparuit hominibus in qua aequalis est Patri."

On the other hand, Gess and Godet, &c., make the gross blunder of confusing "$\mu o \rho \phi \acute{\eta}$"—"form," or "estate"—with "$o \upsilon \sigma \acute{\iota} \alpha$"—"being," or "essence."—as if, indeed, the two were synonymous! Yet surely it is plainly evident that the "$o \upsilon \sigma \acute{\iota} \alpha$" of anything—whether of God, or of one of His creatures—cannot possibly be "laid aside;" inasmuch as It *is* the very *Thing Itself;* while, on the other hand, the "$\mu o \rho \phi \acute{\eta}$" of anything *can* be readily "laid aside;" inasmuch as it is merely an "estate," dependent on its external relations. When our Lord, therefore, became man, He could not possibly relinquish His "$o \upsilon \sigma \acute{\iota} \alpha$"—i. e. *Himself;*—but, on the other hand, could not possibly *fail* to "relinquish" His "$\mu o \rho \phi \acute{\eta}$" of Divinity, and assume in its place His "$\mu o \rho \phi \acute{\eta}$" of humanity; inasmuch as He was now in flesh appearing.

is entirely owing to their oversight, or even definite rejection, of this all important fact that men, like Gess, or Godet, have been enabled to predicate even mistakes and errors to our Lord!

Although, then, He possessed a natural human mind, with all its natural human limitations, yet it was, as I have already stated, perfect in all respects, and without any of the congenital, or acquired imperfections and aberrations that arise from sin; a mind, in short, such as nowhere else was found: and furthermore; It was, I repeat, the Infinite and Omniscient Logos Who was expressing Himself through that mind; expressing Himself to a degree of which we can form but a faint conception.

Take the wisest, the holiest, the best of men, those whose intellects have towered highest over their fellows, or those who have been most fully under the illuminating inspiration of God, take even those holy ones who will, at the consummation of all things, attain to the Beatific Vision of their God, free there from all the distractions and illusions of this time of testing and education, take, I say, the most perfect humanity to which the highest and holiest of us can attain, and this we can surely *at least* predicate of Him Who was called the "Son of Man."[62] If the mind of a Kepler, or a Newton could apprehend the laws of the Universe, how much more capable of that apprehension must have been the human intellect of Him "by Whom all things consist?" If the redeemed ones can know their God in the Beatific Vision, how much more capable of that knowledge must have been the human mind of Him Who is ever in the Bosom of the Father? And although we may demur to the "dicta" of some of the Schoolmen, when they argued that all events—past, present, and future—must have been perfectly known to His human mind,[63] on the ground that such a claim, in all strictness, would imply an Eutychian, or even Monophysitic predication of Omniscience to that finite intellect, yet if we will but consider the foreknowledge that has been displayed by inspired men, we will not be too exacting on this score. He Who inspired the prophets of old, could well, even in His human limitations, know the thoughts of men (St. Matt., ix, 4; xii, 25; St. Mark, ii, 8; St. Luke, v, 22; vi, 8; ix, 47, etc.); say to Nathanael "I saw thee under the figtree" (St. John,

---

(62) Vide St. Thomas [Sum: Theo: Pars iii. Q. ix, art. 2.] "Utrum Christus habuerit scientiam quam habent Beati vel Comprehensores?" affirmed; and so again [Q. idem, art. 3.] "Utrum Christus habuerit scientiam inditam vel infusam, praeter scientiam beatam?" affirmed; thus: "Intellectus autem possibilis humanus est in potentia ad omnia intelligibilia. Reducitur autem in actum per species intelligibiles; quae sunt quaedam formae completivae ipsius." But yet, of course, this knowledge, both "beatific," and "infused," does *not* mean *Omniscience;* but only such "inspired illumination" as our Lord *must* have had in plenary fullness; inasmuch as *He was the Inspirer.* [See pp. 40 and 45, and note 60.]

(63) So Peter Lombard [Liber Sent: Book iii, dist. 14.] "Si anima Christi habuerit sapientiam parem cum Deo, et si omnia scit quae Deus?" Decided in the affirmative; on the ground that "our Lord had the Spirit without measure" [St. John iii, 34]. So too Hugo de S. Victor, Duns Scotus, &c. Yet nevertheless, inasmuch as he [Peter Lombard] also confesses that although Christ knew all things as does God, still "nec ita clare et perspicue omnia capit ut Deus," he probably meant nothing more by the above than the "scientiam inditam vel infusam" of Aquinas.

i, 48); and, in short, on many occasions, give evidence of the possession of knowledge, unattainable to, yet *not incomprehensible* by, unaided and uninspired humanity.⁶⁴

Bearing, then, all these facts in mind, we may say that while our Lord, in His Incarnation, was, it is true, necessarily limited by the medium—the humanity—through which he worked; yet we must not, and dare not deny to Him the fullest powers of which that humanity is capable; nor even such powers and knowledge as it might legitimately be inspired with from on High: and furthermore; while it is true that, in the "humiliation" — the "Kenosis"—of His "local manifestation," His human mind was, no doubt, necessarily "ignorant" of many things that it could not possibly contain, yet it did not, and could not suffer from an error in judgment, or in thought; inasmuch as in it, and through it was working the *Inerrant Logos of God.*⁶⁵

And yet further: our Lord could be *tempted ;* for liability to temptation (although not necessarily to *sin*, as Apollinarius maintained) is inseparable from every human existence. For, if we analyse temptation, we will, I think, find it to be something that is necessarily common to every man; common, not because he is "fallen," but because he is, first of all, both a *self-centered*, and a *finite* being; and secondly, because he is a *man*, made in the "image" of God; and therefore a being to be educated, and developed by temptation into a more perfect likeness.

In the first place, then, temptation is necessarily common to every man, because he both a *self-centered*, and a *finite* being. All material Nature, in so far as it is unconscious, and irresistibly swayed by its "Ultimate Reality"—God,—is, manifestly, outside the range of, and impervious to "temptation." And He Who is its "Underlying Reality," certainly, cannot be tempted; for He, as the All-knowing, cannot be deceived, or misled by anything.

But man, and in fact, all created and finite conscious beings of whatever kind—angels, or dwellers in the stars,⁶⁶—in so far as they are self-conscious and self-centered, and therefore also self determined—possessing in other words, the powers of free thought, and free will—are, just so far, necessarily amenable to "temptation;" and therefore liable (but only *liable*) to fall into sin. For they can, and they must, on many occasions, determine the path that they will tread; and because they are not Omniscient,

---

(64) Thus, for example, He foretold His betrayal, Crucifixion, and Resurrection [St. Matt: xii, 40; xvii, 22, 23; xx, 18, 19; xxvi, 21; St. Mark ix. 31; x, 33, 34; St. Luke ix, 22; xiii, 32, 33; xviii. 31-33; xxii, 21; St. John ii. 19; vi, 70, 71; xii. 32, 33]; the denial of St. Peter [St. Matt. xxvi, 34; St. Mark xiv. 30; St. Luke xxii, 34; St. John xiii, 38]; the destruction of Jerusalem [St Mark xiii; St. Luke xix, 43; xxi, 6]; and the end of the world [St. Matt: xxiv; St. Mark xiii, 24.]

(65) Causing it, therefore, in the language of St. Thomas Aquinas [vide note 62], to possess all the fullness of the "scientia infusa:" Similar, also, is the teaching of St. John Damascene [De Fide Orth: Lib: iii, cap. 21 and 22]. See also the parallel fact of our Lord's Impeccability. [Vide p. 45.]

(66) Vide St. Thomas Aquinas [Sum: Theo: Pars I*a*, Q. lxiii, art. 1.] "Respondeo dicendum, quod tam Angelus quam quaecumque creatura rationalis, si in sua natura consideretur, potest peccare."

but finite in their knowledge, they are, therefore, liable to make mistakes in judgment, choose the wrong path, and ultimately, then, to even fall into sin.[67]

And in the second place, temptation is necessarily common to every man, because he is a being made in the "image" of God; and has therefore to be educated and developed into a more perfect likeness; a work that only temptation and experience can accomplish.

But this second reason is, evidently, closely akin to, and even dependent upon the first, namely the finite knowledge and will of man;[68] and both are well summed up in one by Bishop Butler, in his "Analogy," as follows: "mankind, and perhaps all finite creatures, from the very constitution of their nature, before habits of virtue, are deficient, and in danger of deviating from what is right; and therefore stand in need of virtuous habits for a security against this danger" (Part I, Chap. V, sect. 4).[69]

Temptation, then, springs from our finite manhood; and the great security, therefore, against it, as Bishop Butler here points out, lies in the direction of "habitual righteousness;" or in other words, in the educated ability to resist, slowly acquired through painful experience.

But there is yet another conceivable method of overcoming temptation, namely by an "inspiration" from on High; which "inspiration," again, may take the form, either of an "illumination"—a showing, with more or less clearness, the true inwardness, and final results of the course towards which we are tempted;—or else it may come as an "irresistible guidance," or impulse from God, overbearing the temptation, and rendering it of none effect.

Now in comparing these two (or perhaps, more strictly, these *three*) methods of resisting temptation, it will be noticed then an "inspiration from God" is the more effective one; being absolutely certain in its latter form of an "irresistible impulse"; and only less so in its other form of a "Divine illumination."

On the other hand, an "educated ability to resist," acquired through experience, while certainly giving, at the most, but comparative security, is yet the one best adapted for the ordinary rule of life. For the chief end of man's life on earth being (apparently) to educate him, any rendering sin impossible, by means of an infallible and irresistible guidance, would defeat its own ends. An automaton, swayed by irresistible impulse to do right,

---

(67) For a consideration of the question as to how a "falling short" passes over into *Sin*, see the Essay on "the Essential nature of Sin."
(68) And is, in fact, the "final cause," or reason "ad quem" of temptation, as that first is its "primal cause," or reason "a quo."
(69) St. Clement of Alex: has the same thought when he says that we can attain impeccability by training, until "habit becomes virtue" [Strom: Lib: vii, cap. 7] Compare, also, the old proverb "$\pi a \vartheta \eta \mu a \tau a \; \mu a \vartheta \eta \mu a \tau a$," quoted in Herodotus [Lib: i, 207]; and St. Augustine's words "de vitiis nostris scalam nobis facimus, si vitia ipsa calcamus." [Sermo iii de Ascen.]

such as man, in that case, would be, at the close of such guidance, would not only be quite as impotent, and quite as rudimentary in his spiritual nature as he was in the beginning, but also any gain, arising from the mechanically acquired "habits of virtue," would be more than counterbalanced by such an accompanying atrophy of the will power and spirituality as would inevitably ensue.

Nor even would a protection by "illumination" altogether escape this fatal weakening of man's individuality and spiritual nature; that is if it were a course at all extensively employed, and without a previous willingness to be so "illuminated" on the part of the individual soul. For although the will power and individuality, in such a case, might not, and in fact, would not, be so seriously injured and atrophied as they would be under an "irresistible guidance," yet, I think, they would be injured; for a spirit of moral dependence, and therefore of weakness, would, undoubtedly, be thereby fostered.

True it is that man, having "fallen," and inherited a more or less biased nature, is in need of the "grace"—the "inspired illumination"—of God to overcome, and often to even detect the evil. But this "inspired grace" is always given, I think, merely in relation to a few doubtful points, where "light" or "illumination" is both absolutely necessary, and otherwise unobtainable: and furthermore; it is also always given to a willing subject; and therefore does not come into conflict with, or over-ride the individuality and will. But the consideration of "infused grace" need not detain us here, for the special point I am now making is merely that man, as a self-centered and free-willed finite being, is necessarily subject, by the very fact of his existence, to be "tempted."

And furthermore: man must not only *do* right, but must *be* right—be holy;—must, in other words, learn to hate sin, quâ sin; and to love the right, quâ right; and such a disposition can only be acquired as the result of an education and experience, painful often, and toilsome, but yet abundantly worthy of all the suffering and all the toil.

"Irresistible impulse," then, can find no place in man; and even "Divine guidance by illumination" is only allowable and necessary in relation to those "prima data" that make an education possible—those first springs of knowledge, in other words, upon which all else depends; and where any mistake, or falling short would mean irretrievable ruin to the race.[70] "Prime intuitions"—"infallible inspirations"—from God are restricted, therefore, to those indispensable axioms in ethics (such as the "laws of conscience"), and in thought (such as "necessary truth," mathematical, or logical), upon which all our "knowledge" and "experience" is based; and which (even if such necessary "prime data" could be

---

(70) Vide note 1, and the Essay on "Spirit and Matter."

dispensed with) "experience" could not possibly acquire in time to prevent ruin to mankind.

So again, "infused grace" (as has been already hinted) is, I think, simply and solely a further extension into the realm of the "spiritual" of this inspiration of necessary prime axioms; for just as man needs the axioms of "necessary truth" to make intellectual experience, and even existence possible; and again needs the axioms of "conscience" to make moral life possible; so too does he need the axioms of "infused grace" to make spiritual (as distinguished from, and superior to, moral) life possible." Yet in none of these instances do these "inspired axioms"—intellectual, moral, or spiritual—destroy the free will and individuality of the man; but, on the contrary, are indispensable to both; and that by granting such necessary "prima data" as give the will opportunity to act, and allow experience to be gained.[71]

"Inspired illumination," then, so long as it is confined to these basic axioms, does not destroy, or even injure the will and individuality of man; but on the contrary is, as I have said, the necessary concomitant to both. But these necessary "prima data" having been given, man, as a self-contained and self-limited being, is perforce left to (in some degree) work out his own salvation, win a holy character by the only possible way, namely by overcoming temptation, and thus, in short, "learn by the things that he suffers."

This being so, let us now see the bearing of all this upon the Personality of our Lord—His perfect sinlessness; and yet His real temptation.

In the first place, then, in taking human nature, He necessarily assumed, with its other limitations, this liability to temptation springing from its finiteness. As the Omniscient and Omnipresent Logos He, obviously, could not be "tempted," for He knew all things. But as the Incarnate Logos, "locally limited" by the humanity He had assumed, He could not, with His human intellect, comprehend all things; and consequently, then, *could be tempted*.

And even further: not only was He tempted because of His human limitations, but also in order that He—the Son of Man—

---

(71) Vide St. Thomas Aquinas [Sum: Theo: Pars ia, 2ae, Q. cx, art. 1.] "Gratia est quaedam *lux* animae;" and again [Q. idem, art. 3.] "Ut naturale lumen rationis aliquid est praeter virtutes acquisitas; ita supernaturale gratiae lumen sive donum, est aliquid praeter virtutes infusas quibus homo perficitur ad ambulandum, secundum quod congruit divinae gratiae lumini."

Similarly, according to the Fathers, "grace" is an *added* gift to the natural man, lost by the "fall," and restored by the Incarnation; and is, in short, in no sense, in *negation*, or *opposition* to "nature;" but, on the contrary, is rather its *restoration*. Vide St. Athanasius [De Incar: Verbi Dei, § 4]; St. Clement of Alex: [Strom: Lib: vi, cap. 12]; St. Irenaeus [Contra Haer: Lib: iv, cap. 38]; St. Augustine [De Spiritu et Littera, xxvii, 47]: &c.

Agreeable also to this is what I have pointed out, in chap. I of this Treatise, concerning the incomplete and prophetic character of man's nature; inasmuch as it points upwards to, and is only fulfilled in, the Incarnation.

(72) The consideration of this necessity of "prime data" for the operations of is "free will," will clearly show us the close inter-dependence—*not opposition*—there a between the guidings of the Omnipotent, and the workings of our will.

might experience to the full all our nature—might, in other words, even as we do, "learn by the things that He suffered" (Heb. v, 7),—and so be a merciful and faithful High Priest, Who could be, to the fullest extent, sympathetic with us His brethren. He was, then, "tempted on all points like as we are, yet without sin"—tempted both as a true man, and as our Elder Brother;—and that to a degree such as we can hardly imagine. For He possessed, as I have already stated (pp. 36 *et seq.*), a perfect humanity, without any of the marrings or imperfections arising from sin, congenital, or acquired; and was, therefore, endowed with the most perfect and exquisite sensibilities; and therefore, again, could, as I have said, feel the poignancy of temptation to a degree we can hardly realize.

For the "agony of temptation" can hardly be said to have much meaning to an unholy and impure man; and it is only so far as we strive to do right, and are possessed, in some measure, with the spirit of holiness, that such an expression has any fitness: so, again, does refinement of nature and disposition count for much; a civilised man is "tempted" far more than a savage, and a gentleman than a boor. In short the more perfect and highly organised a being is, the more numerous are his relations to the Universe, and the fuller, therefore, is his life; and therefore, also, the more numerous and powerful are his temptations (if he be finite); and the more grievous and deadly his sin, if he falls.

If this be true, then how exquisitely sensitive, in every direction, must have been the human nature of Him Who was both the holiest and the most refined of all the sons of men? True, He could never have known one fearful class of temptations, namely those sins that assault us with the awful prestige of former victories, and of "habit;" and to overcome which we have, in a special sense, to fight against ourselves. But although He knew not this terrible uprooting of "habitual sin," yet He did know, in His exquisitely perfect humanity, all the sensibilities, and even (if we may so speak) the weaknesses to which these sins appeal; and He further knew the conflict with the far more subtle, and seductive temptations that arise from apparent, or at the utmost, only *incomplete* right—the doing of a "little evil," or of a "rather doubtful" act, that "great good" might ensue—the exercising, in short, of a "little wise diplomacy," such as men sometimes commend to us;—for on one occasion, at least, was this momentary bowing to evil asked of Him, in return for the Kingship over the souls of men (St. Matt., iv, 9; St .Luke, iv, 7).

Such, then, were our Lord's temptations; far more subtle, more intense, more acute than any we may have to endure; even after allowing for the non-presence in His experience of temptation from "habitual sin." How, then, it may be asked, was He enabled to endure; and especially how was He able, while being thus vitally tempted, to yet remain "without sin"?

To fully answer this question it is necessary to again refer to the human nature of our Lord. In man, as has already been stated, we have an "Ego," a mental life, and a bodily life with a body; altogether forming one self contained individuality—a man. And, as again has been stated, because a man is this self contained individuality, the utmost inspired aid to live right that can be given him can only come in the form of an "illumination" from God; which "illumination" must not exceed the necessary "initial data" of life, under penalty of injuring the said individuality.

But in our Lord and Saviour Christ we have, as has already been laid down (pp. 23, 24), no human "Ego;" but He Himself—the Logos—is the "Ego" of His humanity; creating around Him (so to speak) the real mental life, bodily life, and body of a man; being thus really Incarnate, thus the true God-man.

The "inspired guidance," therefore, that with a human "Ego" would be limited to an "illumination" of prime intuitional truth, with Him was not so limited, nor indeed could be, for the *Inspirer was Himself.*[13] On the one hand, then, no atrophy of, or injury to His individuality was to be feared; and on the other, the "mechanical habit of virtue" (so to speak), resulting to His humanity from this "Infallible Guidance," was itself the necessary education of that humanity; for only thus was it perfectly moulded to His will.

And this brings us to the question of the "Two Wills" of our Lord, a doctrine of the Catholic faith that was enforced against the Monothelites (pp. 21, 22), who upheld, it will be remembered, the "$\mu o\nu \acute{\epsilon}\rho\gamma\epsilon\iota\alpha$" or "One Will" of our Lord. Yet, at the first sight, this contention of the Monothelites seems perfectly accurate; for if we analyse, as far as may be, our own being, we will, I think, find that "will" is the center and core of personality itself—is, in other words, the prime essential note of individuality, and of a differentiation from the external world. A "will," then, and an "Ego" are entirely correlated terms; and where there is but one "Ego," there can be, properly speaking, but one will. Since our Lord, then, was *One Person*, although possessing Two Natures, His "will," strictly speaking, was but *One* also; and the Monothelites, who argued similarly, were quite correct in so doing; but yet the conclusions that they drew from these premises, namely that our Lord's humanity was therefore devoid of a proper human will, were, obviously, entirely wrong; for a humanity without a "will" would be as Doketic and unreal as one without "thought;" and the vital reality of the Incarnation would thus be lost sight of, and denied!

---

[13] Vide St. Thomas Aquinas ! Sum: Theo: Pars iii, Q. xv, art. 2.] "Cum in Christo virtus cum gratia fuerit secundum perfectissimum gradum, nullo modo fuit in ipso fomes peccati."

Our Lord, therefore, possessed a plenary inspiration of "grace," as well as the plenitude of the "scientia indita vel infusa." [See note 62.]

The solution of this puzzle lies in the full recognition of our Lord's Incarnation as a "*local manifestation and limitation.*" He, in His Eternal Omnipresence, was the Omnipotent Willer of all; but, in His finite and local humanity, He was (as has been already laid down) evidently *limited* by the nature He assumed: as, then, He could not "know" all, so He could not "will" all; for He, certainly, could as little exercise Omnipotence, as Omniscience, while working through a real humanity. He possessed, then, if we may so express it, a *dual state of will*, One Omnipotent in the Logos, One limited in man: if, therefore, we think of the *Oneness of the Willer*—think, in other words, of the "will" as a note of personality—we may say that His Will was *One;* but if, on the other hand, we think of His *Two Natures*—think, in other words, of the "will" as an operation—then we may say that He had *Two Wills*.⁷⁴

And, in fact, this is the key to the whole question; for what the Monothelites insisted on was, not so much the Oneness of the Willer (which, indeed, all allowed), but rather the Oneness of the "ἐνέργεια" or "operation; which "ἐνέργεια" was the Divine Will *alone;* so that the humanity, being thought of as without any "ἐνέργεια," was, in effect, reduced to an Eutychian desuetude.

But perhaps, analysing still deeper, while there were "Two Wills" in the Logos—One Omnipotent, as has just been stated, in the Godhead, and One limited in man,—yet there were not, it seems to me, properly speaking, "Two Wills" in *Christ*— i. e. the *Logos Incarnate*, — but "One Will," or "ἐνέργεια" only; which sole "ἐνέργεια" was His "human Will"—or, speaking more accurately, His Divine Will as working through, and limited by His humanity,—and that alone.⁷⁵

---

(74) Vide St. John Damascene [De Fide Orth: Lib: iii, cap. 14.] "'Επειδὴ τοίνυν εἷς μεν ὁ Χριστός και μία αὐτοῦ ἡ ὑπόστασις, εἷς και ὁ αὐτος ἔστιν ὁ θέλων θεϊκῶς τε και ἀνθρωπίνως and again [De Duabus Voluntatibus.§ 27.] Ἐπειδὴ δε μία τοῦ Χριστοῦ ἡ ὑπόστασις, και εἷς ὁ Χριστός, εἷς ὁ θέλων κατ' ἀμφω τὰς φύσεις.

And so, again, St. Thomas Aquinas [Sum: Theo: Pars iii, Q xviii, art. 1.] "Utrum in Christo sint duae voluntates." * * * "Respondeo dicendum quod quidam posuerunt in Christo esse unam solam voluntatem. Sed ad hoc ponendum diversimode moti esse videntur;" and goes on to argue that "will" is an essential to the human reason; and is therefore indispensable to the humanity of our Lord.

(75) St. John Damascene [De Fide Orth: Lib: iii, cap. 14.] " τότε γαρ ταῦτα φυσικῶς ἤθελεν ὅτε ἡ θεία αὐτοῦ θέλησις ἤθελε ,και παρεχώρει τῇ σαρκι πάσχειν και πράττειν τα ἴδια."

CHAPTER VI

OUR Lord, then, as we have seen, in His earthly manifestation as the Incarnate One, could be both "ignorant," and "tempted;" and that in a real and vital manner; for the finite humanity He there assumed must needs have been so limited, have so suffered, and so too have been educated for Himself; but yet, although thus limited, He could neither be mistaken, nor fall into sin; and that because He, the "Ego" and Inspirer of that humanity, was the Omniscient and All Holy Logos of God; "locally limited," it is true, in His "manifestation," by its proper finite limitations; but yet, certainly, loosing nothing thereby of His own Essential Holiness and Infinitude.

And this now brings us to another consideration, namely the value of our Lord's life to us as "our Example," a fact that is repeatedly insisted upon in the New Testament[76] as an important, although secondary, aspect of His Life.

Yet some may ask of what possible value to us, as an *example*, was that unique life? For He was the Incarnate Logos of God, redeeming and atoning for mankind; and therefore, as some may say, to neither His Person, nor His work, can our lives have any analogy.

In a sense, no doubt, all this is, to some extent, true; and yet, on the other hand, was it not our Lord's primary purpose, in His Incarnation, to be a *perfect man;* and as such, and the great Head of our race, to draw us unto, and unite us with the Father; and only incidentally (so to speak), and in the accomplishment of this end, to redeem us from corruption and sin?

But if this be true, and, indeed, who can deny it, then surely He presents, as our Archetypal and Perfect Head, the closest likeness of what our lives, at least, ought to be; and is, therefore, plainly "our Example." And even further: not only is there this close analogy to us, in His Person as the Archetypal man, so that we have clear exemplars for our conduct in His perfect Life, but we even, as I hope to show, have some real share and fellowship in His supremest work, namely the redemption of, and atonement for mankind.

In fact we may lay it down as a cardinal axiom that *whatever our Lord wrought in His Incarnation, that He evidently wrought as the Incarnate One; and therefore as man, and as man alone.* There was, then, in Him, as has been already remarked (p. 29),

---

(76) Vide Romans xv, 5; Philip: ii, 5; I St. Peter ii, 21. See also St. Matt: xi, 29; St. John xiii, 15; &c.

no alternation of parts—no acting sometimes as God, and sometimes as a man,—but a constant and unvarying living, in all respects, the life of the Archetypal Head of our race: this is evidently a most important fact, and one that is too often forgotten in many expositions of our Lord's life."

He was, then, as I have said, in all the circumstances of His life and work, our "Example;" and that too, as I have already hinted, and will hereafter more fully show, even in those things, such as His miraculous powers, and especially His atoning death, that may seem, at the first sight, most alien to our natures.

Our *Example*, I say, not our *Pattern*;⁷⁸ for while we certainly cannot be Catholic Christs—Incarnate "Logoi" of God,—yet we can, and ought to be (so to speak) *Nestorian Ones*—"Θεοφόροι—, or be, in other words, men inspired and indwelt by Him, Who will guide our actions, and lead us home.

And yet, as I have already remarked (pp. 42, 43), this inspiring guidance — this "grace" — will be no "irresistible impulse," atrophying our wills, and rendering us useless automata; but will rather be an extension of the "Light" that lighteneth every man; a power, therefore, to recognise and resist the hidden temptations of evil. While our wills, then, will, in no sense, be atrophied or impaired; but will rather be given opportunities for action; yet our natures will be trained to "habitual righteousness" by that indwelling and inspiring Spirit of God; working in us, as we are willing, and drawing us nearer to God.

Our Lord, then, was our "Example," in His earthly life; both as manifesting to us the general character of a Divinely guided life; and even more particularly, as I will proceed to show, as setting before us the results of inspiration from the Holy Spirit; but before passing on to this point, let us first consider, as briefly as may be, another respect in which our Lord, as the "Primal Adam"—the "Archetypal Man,"—is our Example of what, at least, we *might* have been, were it not for the ruin wrought in us by sin; I refer, in short, to His Transfiguration.

This event, as we know, is said by St. Paul (Philip: iii, 21) to be an example of the glories of the resurrection body—a manifestation of what shall be for the pure and holy⁷⁹; and it has, therefore, been further expounded, and apparently satisfactorily, as

---

(77) Which oversight, as I may remark, is a mistake made by most of the Christological heresies [especially those modern ones of the school of Gess]; and springs, it seems to me, from their common initial mistake of conceiving of our Lord's humanity as having a separate and previous existence, before He "assumed" it: vide pp. 23, 24, and note 34.

(78) Parallel to this thought is what St. Thomas Aquinas says, when discussing whether our Lord suffered, in His Passion, all varieties of human agonies; thus: "passus est Christus omnes passiones humanes, non quidem secundum speciem, sed secundum genus." [Sum: Theo: Pars iii, Q. xlvi, art. 5.]

(79) This is the aspect of the Transfiguration, principally touched upon by the Fathers and Schoolmen: Vide St. Leo the Great [Sermo ii, 3]; St. Basil [Hom: in Psl: xliv, 2]; St. Augustine [Exp: ad Gal:]; Theodoret [Epist: cxlv]; St. Gregory the Great [Moral: Lib: xxxii, cap. 6]; St. Anselm [Hom: iv]; Peter Lombard [Liber Sent: Book iii, dist. 16, q. 2, art. 1]; St. Thomas Aquinas [Sum: Theo: Pars iii, Q. xlv, art. 2, ad. 3]; &c.

an example of what would have been, had not sin come into the world, the natural ending of the earthly life of unfallen and perfect man. In such a case, it is said, there would have been no pangs of dissolution—no fierce grapple with death, our last dread foe,—but "the natural body" would have faded into the "spiritual" one—life be swallowed up in a larger life;—without the previous suffering and ignominy of death and the tomb.

But man having "fallen," and become a sinner, by that "fall" and sin is subjected to the dark mystery of death; so that his body can no longer be "clothed upon," but must first pass through corruption and the grave. Yet hints of the glories that might have been are occasionally given, as in the shining of the face of Moses, the fiery chariot of Elijah, and above all, the Transfiguration of our Lord.

Yet the consummation of this glory—this natural ending of His perfect human life—He deliberately renounced; and preferring to be made in all things like unto His brethren, in order to redeem them from their sin, set His face towards Jerusalem, went on to His Passion and the grave, and tasted death for every man.

Our Lord, then, I repeat, was, in all respects, our "Example;" and that both as manifesting to us the capabilities of a perfect human nature; and also as illustrating what a perfect man—one holy, loving, and inspired by God—should be: and this leads us on to the question of His Inspiration by the Holy Ghost.

No one, who has studied at all carefully the Gospel record of our Lord, will deny that many things in His life are spoken of as done under the inspiration and guidance of the Holy Spirit of God. Thus He is "filled with the Spirit" at His Baptism;[80] He is led up by the same Spirit into the wilderness to be "tempted of the devil;"[81] He declares at the beginning of His ministry "the Spirit of the Lord is upon me;"[82] and finally all His miracles are declared to have been performed, not by His own Power, but by that of the Inspiring Spirit."

Now all these things, and especially His Baptism, and Wonder working by the Spirit, were certainly no more Doketic "seemings"—mere actings to the world;—for such an interpretation would both eviscerate those actions of any real meaning; and would also blasphemously fasten the charge of deliberate falsehood upon the Holy and True.

Yet, on the other hand, since He is the Logos—God of God, and Light of Light, of One Essence with the Father,—we may possibly fail to see the precise necessity for, or indeed meaning in, such an Inspiration by that Holy Spirit, Who Himself "Proceedeth through the Son."

And no mere consideration of the Oneness of the Godhead, and

---
(80) St. Matt:iii. 16; St. Mark i. 10; St. Luke iii. 22; St. John I. 33.
(81) St. Matt:iv. 1; St Mark i. 12; St. Luke iv. 1.
(82) St. Luke iv. 18; vide also verse 14.
(83) St. Matt:xii. 28; St. Luke v. 17; xi. 20; St. John xiv. 12; Acts x. 38.

the Equality in action of the Triune Persons, will help us here; for the question is, not why the Holy Spirit should act (for, indeed, both He, and the Father must ever act), but why He should be the *Inspirer*—why, in short, the Son should be, in some sense, *inert;* needing, therefore, to be baptised with, be led by, and work His miracles through, Him?

The answer to this question will, I am sure, again be found in that necessary "Kenosis" or "self emptying"—that "local limitation," consequent upon the medium of His Incarnation, namely, His humanity,—of which I have already treated.

For the Logos, certainly, in the Omnipresent Estate of His Godhead, needed no inspiration, or guidance by the Holy Spirit, other than that necessary "circumincession" and co-working proper to the Blessed Trinity.

But in the "local manifestation" of the Logos—the Incarnation—He was, as I have repeatedly stated, necessarily limited by the capabilities of the nature He assumed; for His humanity, being real and natural, manifestly possessed only human powers and capabilities; albeit these were perfect of their kind. It was, then, evidently impossible for Him to perform superhuman acts, or miracles by that humanity's means; He could only do these works by means of the non-Incarnate, Unconfined, and Infinite Divine Power; or in other words, by the Inspiration of that same Holy Spirit, Who is the Inspirer of all the children of God; so that our Lord was, even in this respect, as in all others, acting as Very Man, and as our "Example."

And this shows us the meaning of, and necessity for, the Baptism of our Lord; which, I emphatically repeat, was no mere Doketic acting to the world; but had, on the contrary, a real and vital meaning. Before that rite He, in His Incarnation, possessed but human powers; and while He waited, the mysteries of that Incarnation, and of His redemption were hid in silence from the world.[84]

But when the time was come[85] that He should proclaim liberty to the captive, and redemption to the sons of men, then it became necessary that He, the Opener of a New Dispensation — the Bearer of a new Revelation,—should possess the power of working miracles or "signs," as the tokens of, and authentic vouchers for His Mission from on High.[86]

---

(84) Vide what is said on p. 33 concerning the "secretness" of the Virgin Birth.

(85) Vide St. John ii, 11, "this *beginning* of miracles, &c." This consideration, as was pointed out by St. Chrysostom [Super Joan: Hom: xvij], who is, again, quoted by St. Thomas Aquinas [Sum: Theo: Pars iii, Q. xliii, art. 3, ad. 1], effectually disposes of all the pseudo miracles of the various apocryphal and heretical "Gospels of the Infancy," &c.

(86) Vide St. Thomas Aquinas [Sum: Theo: Pars iii, Q. xliii, art. 1.] "Respondeo dicendum quod Divinitus conceditur homini miracula facere propter duo. Primo quidam et principaliter ad confirmandam veritatem quam aliquis docet" * * * "ut dum aliquis facit opera quae solus Deus facere potest, credantur ea quae dicuntur esse a Deo.," * * * 'Secundo, ad ostendendam praesentiam Dei in homine per gratiam Spiritus Sancti: ut dum scilicet homo facit opera Dei, credatur Deus habitare in eo per gratiam."

He therefore wrought, as I have said, His miracles or "signs," not by the power of His own Incarnate Godhead (which, because *Incarnate*, was powerless to work them); but solely as the prophets of God have ever wrought them, namely by the power of that Holy Spirit, Who was given to Him in all Plenitude from His Baptism (St. John, iii, 34); and therefore, again, not as illustrating His own Power—as setting forth Himself;[87]—but, as I have stated, simply as the gift of God—as tokens of, and vouchers for, His Mission from the Father.

We will now pass on to the very difficult subject of the prayers of our Lord; and will consider, as briefly, and yet as accurately as may be, how, and in what sense, our Lord could be said to "pray."

Many find great difficulty in conceiving such a thing: that ignorant and sinful men should be said to "pray" to God—should request favors from Him,—this, they say, is quite intelligible; but that the Incarnate Son—Incarnate, too, by His own Will—should ever be said to "pray"—should ever, in other words, be said to need and request aught from Him, with Whom He is Eternally One,—this, to their mind, is utterly incomprehensible!

But let us, before attempting to solve this question, first define what is the true nature of prayer; and that having been done, we can then more clearly and intelligently decide how, and in what sense, our Lord could really "pray."

Prayer, then, may be considered under two very different, and yet quite coherent aspects; for it may be thought of either as (1) a request or petition for a favour from God (which is almost, to many people, the sole meaning of "prayer"), or else it may be (2) simply a loving communing with our Father—a raising of our hearts to Him, with no very definite petition, save for His presence.

And these two divisions may be again subdivided, according as the prayer is a petition (a) for a gift, (b) for information, or (c) for deliverance from evil; or again, is either a communing (a) personal, and private, or (b) public, and witnessing before others.

Taking first the "communing" aspect of prayer, and that in its "private" variety, we may say that such an act would be most congruous with our Lord's Nature, both as Very God, and as Very Man. For He Who is Eternally in the Bosom of the Father, must ever hold this intercommunion with Him; and even the "local limitations" incident upon the Incarnation were, manifestly, powerless to alter or affect this loving intercourse of the Persons in the Triune God.

But if this "private communing" aspect of prayer is most congruous to the Godhead of our Lord, and even to that Godhead as limited by the Incarnation, not less is it also congruous to His

---

(87) Vide St. John v, 19 and 30 et seq.; viii, 28; xii, 44 et seq.; xiv, 10 et seq.; &c.

true and essential manhood. For every human being that exists, both because he is a creature of God, and is further in the "image" of the Logos, is entitled to come to his Creator saying "our Father;" and Christianity, in its covenant of Baptism, only re-enforces this relationship; and makes us, by that Sacramental Oath, which swears us into the army of the Lord—His Church,—only the more definitely "children" of our Lord.

Our Lord, then, I repeat, could commune with His Father, not only as the "Son," or even as the "Incarnate Son," but also as the "Son of Man;" and could thus, in short, be our Priestly Intercessor, pleading as our Mediator with the Father, because He was truly of One Nature with both God and man.

It is in full accordance with this view that we find so many of the recorded prayers of our Lord to be of this "private communing" character; as for instance His great intercessory prayer, mentioned in the xvii chapter of St. John's Gospel.[88]

But the other variety of "communing prayer" is given us in what I may term the "teaching prayers" of our Lord, wherein He uses this communing as a witness to, and testimony of, His Divine Mission from the Father. Thus at the raising of Lazarus He prayed, thanking His Father, "that they who stood by might believe" (St. John, xi, 42); and of this same character was His prayer in the Temple Courts shortly preceding His Passion (St. John, xii, 30).

I need hardly say that these "teaching" prayers were, in no sense, Doketic unrealities; but were rather, as I have said, "testimonies"—"manifestations" and "signs"—to the world, like the Voices that were heard at His Baptism and Transfiguration, or even like His miracles themselves.

And furthermore; as in the more private "communings," so also may we say here, that this variety of prayer is proper, not less to His humanity, than His Divinity; for we find similar prayers spoken by Moses,[89] by Samuel,[90] by Elijah,[91] and by other prophets of God; the only apparent essential being that the speakers must be true and legitimate ambassadors from Him. This "testimony of mission" was, then, proper, not only to our Lord's Divinity, and that by reason of His Essential Unity with the Father; but also to His humanity, and that by reason of its proper assumption by Him.

Our Lord, then, could pray, in the sense of "communing" with His Father; and that both as Very and True God, and as very and true man; and that again, not only in a private and personal fashion, but also publicly, and as a witnessing to the world: it

---

(88) It should also be noticed that both this class of prayers, and those of the Agony in the Garden, are so evidently personal and private, that they can only have become known to the Evangelists by subsequent revelation; a revelation that was, very probably, made to them by our Lord during the great forty days preceding His Ascension.
(89) Ex: xiv, 15; Numb: xx, 10; &c.
(90) I Sam: xii, 17.
(91) I Kings xviii, 36, 37.

remains now to be seen if he could also be said to "pray," in the sense of making a petition to God.

But "petitionary prayer," as has already been remarked, can be again subdivided, according as it is a petition (a) for a gift, (b) for information, or (c) for deliverance from evil. True it is that these varieties are closely interconnected in many ways; yet, none the less, they are also widely different in some, at least, of their bearings.

Thus taking the first subdivision, it is evident that our Lord could not ask for a gift from His Father, for He possessed all things; and although He had, in His Incarnation, made Himself "poor," that He might "make many rich," yet it was a *voluntary* impoverishment; and any prayer, therefore, for enrichment, even in His Incarnate limitations, and still less in His Essential Godhead, was, manifestly, out of the question.

But, it may yet be asked, would not such a prayer be quite conceivable of, and coherent with, our Lord's finite humanity? Granting that in His Essential Godhead, and even in that Godhead as limited by the Incarnation, He could have no possible need; and therefore, also, could not, in any sense, be said to ask for the fulfillment of a need; yet was not His real and finite humanity capable of such a need; and therefore also capable of making such a prayer?

In answer to this we may point out, first, that our Lord's humanity was the creation of His "Hypostatic" Godhead—was, in short, the *expression* (if we may so speak) of that Incarnate Godhead,—and therefore was not capable of originating any prayer; and secondly, that although it was certainly finite and limited (being real); yet it was none the less, also *perfect;* being both plenarily inspired by the "Hypostatic" Logos with all the *natural* powers and faculties of which it was capable (pp. 35, 36, 39, 40, and 46); and also plenarily endowed by the Holy Spirit with all the superhuman powers it might require (pp. 50 and 51). Even then, in relation to the finiteness of our Lord's humanity, no necessary requirement was left unfulfilled; and any prayer, therefore, for enrichment, even on this score, was totally out of the question.

It is in accordance, we may notice, with this view that when our Lord was tempted by Satan in the wilderness to turn stone into bread for His need (which act would practically involve a "prayer for enrichment"), He refused, saying "man shall not live by bread alone," or as He elsewhere expressed it, His bread was "to do the will of Him that sent Him."

But if any "prayer for enrichment" was utterly alien to His Being, so also was any "request for information." For although He, the Omniscient Logos, was Incarnate in man; and therefore necessarily limited, and "ignorant" of many things; yet (as was remarked in connection with a "prayer for enrichment") He was both *voluntarily* Incarnate, and His humanity was also a *perfect* one, and inspired by the "Hypostatic" Logos with all the knowledge, and all the powers, it was capable of receiving.

It follows, then, as in the previous case, that any "prayer for information" would also be alien to His Nature, alien both as He is Very and True God, and is very and true man; and alien, again, in the latter connection, both by the voluntariness of His limitation, and by the perfect natural knowledge of the humanity He assumed.

It remains, finally, to be seen if He could pray for "deliverance from evil;" and if we examine the records of our Lord's earthly life, we will, I think, find one clear instance of such a prayer, namely in that dread and mysterious scene in the Garden, when He prayed in bitter anguish "Father, if it be possible, let this cup pass from Me; nevertheless not as I will, but as Thou wilt."

Such a bitter cry of human suffering, and human ignorance was, evidently, not the voicing of the Divinity of our Lord, but rather of His real humanity. Certainly as the Eternal Logos of God He could not pray in such terms to the Father; and especially would it be meaningless for Him to say "not as I will, but as Thou wilt;" for in the Godhead that Will is One.

But in the humanity He assumed as the Incarnate One—a humanity that, as I have already shown, was limited, ignorant, emotional, passible, and possessed of the faculty of a human will,—He could thus pray; for that humanity, on the one hand, could not possibly fathom the depths of the Council of God; and on the other, must perforce shrink from the horrible suffering and agony seen before it." Our Lord, therefore, as Very Man, both could, and must pray "if it be possible, let this cup pass from Me;" while from His Divine Will, inspiring that manhood, came yet the further cry "Thy will be done."⁹³

Our Lord, then, both could, and did pray for deliverance from evil; yet it was not in the relation of His Essential Godhead; but in His relation as Incarnate in man.

And I would here like to point out how all the foregoing entirely bears out the Canon I have laid down (p. 47) as to our Lord's continually acting, during His whole Incarnation, as Very Man, and our "Example;" and not working alternately, sometimes as God, and sometimes as man: for, as we have seen, while some of His prayers, such as those of the "communing" variety, are quite predicable of His Godhead; yet *all* are entirely predicable to

---

(92) i. e. by *inspirational* knowledge: vide pp. 39 and 40.
(93) Vide St. Athanasius ["Contra Arian:" Orat; iii, § 29]: St. Chrysostom [Hom: in Matt: lxxxiii, § 1]; St. Leo [Sermo: lvi, 2; and lxvi, 8]; St. Hilary [" De Trin: Lib: x, cap. 37-39.] " Impossibile tamen homini est passionis terrore non vinci, nec possit nisi per probationem fides nesci. Atque ideo et pro hominibus ut homo vult calicem transire, et ut Dei ex Deo voluntas effectui paternae voluntatis unitur" [cap. 18]: St John Damascene [De Fide Orth: Lib: iii, cap. 24.] " ὡς μὲν Θεὸς ταυτοτελὴς ὢν τῷ Πατρὶ ὡς δὲ ἄνϑρωπος τὸ τῆς ἀνϑρωπότητος φυσικῶς ἐνδείκνυται ϑέλημα τοῦτο γὰρ φυσικῶς παραιτεῖται τὸν ϑάνατον."

His manhood; and *some*, as the petition in the Garden just mentioned, are predicable of His manhood *alone*.

Yet another point we might notice is the close connection that all these aspects of our Lord's life, that were manlike alone, have with His Cross and Passion; and in fact, as we may remark, it was during that last Agony and Passion of our Lord that His real humanity was most apparent; not, of course, that He was more human, during that period, than on any other occasion; but simply that the sufferings of the Garden, and of the Cross, showed the more passible, and evidently human side, both of His human body, and of the human emotions of His mind.

And this brings us to the most awful and most mysterious of all our Lord's sayings, namely that most bitter lament upon the cross, when He cried, amidst the thick darkness, "My God! My God! why hast Thou forsaken Me!!"

But taking even the lowest, and most heretical view of our Lord's Person, and considering Him simply as a great prophet of God, how, it may well be asked, could these words be true—how, in short, could the Father be said, in any sense, to have forsaken the Righteous? While if we hold the Catholic faith, and believe Him to be, not merely man, but the Incarnate Logos of God, we may well wonder in what possible sense our Lord could give this cry.

In the Omnipresent Estate of the Logos He certainly was inseparable from the Father; and He evidently was not less so in His earthly manifestation as the Christ; while His humanity alone could not have willed this cry: for not only was that humanity "impersonal," and without a human "Ego" (pp. 23 and 24); but still further, if such an interpretation of the cry were true, then there must have been, at that moment, a *separation* between the humanity and the Divinity; and the Incarnation, in short, as the Gnostics taught (vide p. 16), must then have *ceased to be!* It is, then, utterly incredible that either the Logos "Ego," or the human nature alone, could have volunteered this cry; and yet it evidently had a meaning, and that a most awful one; for even apart from the falsity of any mere Doketic "acting," His agony and woe were too evidently sincere and heartfelt—the cry was too evidently wrung from the abyss of His anguish—for any other supposition to be, for a moment, tenable.

But although the "impersonal" human nature *alone* could not have willed that cry, yet it evidently only had a meaning in relation to that human nature; and the solution is, probably, to be found in the following considerations.

As I have already remarked (p. 36), our Lord, in assuming humanity, took with it, not only the clear and cold reasoning powers of the intellect, but also those warmer, and more individualised faculties of the emotions that help to make a perfect man. As a Possessor, then, of this emotional nature He could enter, to the fullest extent, not only into our affections and sympathies, but also into our sufferings and woes; and that, too, in all their sharpness and intensity.

For, as already has been remarked (p. 44) with reference to temptation, the higher and more refined the type of a man, and the fuller, therefore, is his life, the more acutely, also, will he feel the power of temptation: and so, again, may we say that the more perfect a man—the more refined, imaginative, and full of life he is,—the greater also will be his realisation of the grim horror of death.

True, he may, by summoning all his will power and resolution, simply refuse to face that horror; and thus, preserving his nerves unshattered, meet death with unflinching fortitude. And so, again, may the Christian, in the hour of death, strengthen himself by trust in his Saviour; and although this trust does not, in any way, lessen the horribleness of death, yet it draws our mind away to the greater glories to come, so that the fear of death is, not, indeed, destroyed, but "swallowed up in victory."

But while, then, our Lord, as the Perfect Man, was most keenly alive, and keenly responsive in every fibre of His Being to every human emotion and sensation; and therefore, again, was sensible, to the fullest possible extent, of all the poignancy of the horror of death that the natural man could feel; yet nevertheless, as our Representative—as the great Son of Man,—He steadfastly refused to either turn His eyes away from that horror, or to deaden His sensibilities by partaking of the proffered myrrh; but, on the contrary, drank His cup of bitterness to the very dregs; suffering therein, to the fullest extent, all that man could ever know—"tasting death for every man."

And yet again; as He deliberately faced that horror in all its bitterness, putting aside both the merciful anodyne, and the stoical nerving of oneself by simply refusing to think of it (courses which although quite allowable, and even commendable to us, would not be suitable to Him, as the Representative Man), as, I say, He deliberately faced that horror, so too He could not take the comfort of the believer, and let death be "swallowed up in victory;" for His work at that moment was, not to minimise, but to taste that bitterness of death in all its natural fullness.

If we consider for a moment we will, I think, find that the most awful horror the mind of man can shudderingly conceive is that of blank desolation in the midst of unfathomable space. Compared with this terror all the pangs of Dante's fancied Inferno are almost as nothing; for they, at least, had the solace of company and fellowship. And with this supreme horror the terrors of dissolution are closely akin; for, in that dread hour, we feel ourselves irresistibly slipping into the dark abyss of death, with our friends and loved ones powerless to accompany or aid, as, naked and solitary, we pass to our doom.

True, as I have said, with the Christian, this horror is overcome, and this solitariness relieved by the faith in our Risen Redeemer; but, as I have again said, in His own last Agony, no such relief was possible, for He was dying as the great "Son of Man"—"treading the wine press alone,"—and none there was to help Him.

As, then, the blackness of dissolution stole upon Him, and His soul was suffering the keenest pangs of which humanity is capable, who can wonder that from that human soul was wrung the awful cry of supremest anguish—that the sense of desolation overcame it,—and that He exclaimed "Why hast Thou forsaken Me!"

Not that it was, of course, in any sense true that there actually was this forsakeness; but simply that the sensations His soul was then experiencing could be given expression in no other way; for although the Presence was the same, yet the *sense* of that Presence was becoming dim and uncertain to the human soul; and the growing feeling of desolation could be voiced in no other manner: thus, as it has been well expressed, "non solvit unionem, sed subtraxit visionem;" a "subtraction" that was not, of course, in any sense, on the part of God; but, simply and solely, a want of realisation, as I have said, on the part of the human soul; whose eye of perception was then being glassed over by the icy hand of death.

It was, then, if we may so express it, the cry of dying humanity that our Lord was thus voicing as our Supreme Head; *voicing* it, I say, not as the expression of His own individuality, but as the "Son of Man."[94]

And yet this "voicing" partook, in no sense, of the nature of a Doketic "seeming;" for although it was, obviously, not true of His complete Person, yet it *was* true, in a sensational sense, of His emotional nature: in accordance with this idea, I think, is the fact that it was a quotation by our Lord from the xxii Psalm—that it was not, in other words, original with Him, but was the utterance, long before, of a suffering human soul.

---

(94) Vide the Epistle to the Hebrews; and especially chap. v, 7, 8; St. Athanasius [De Incar: Contra Arian: § 2.] "ἐκ προσώπου ἡμετέρου λέγει;" and [Orat: contra Arian: iii, cap. 10; and iv, cap. 2]; St. Gregory Nazianzen [Orat: xxx. 5.] "οὐ γαρ αὐτὸς ἐγκαταλέλειπται" . . . . "ἐν ἑαυτῷ δε, ὅπερ εἶπον, τύποι το ἡμέτερον;" St. Augustine [Epist: cxl, § 6.] "Haec ex persona sui corporis Christus dicit, quod est Ecclesia:" and [Com: in Psl: xxi. 1; 2nd Exp]; St John Damascene [De Fide Orth: Lib: iii, cap. 24.] "ὥστε το ἡμέτερον οἰκειούμενος προσώπον ταῦτα προσηύξατο." Vide also Theodoret [Com: in Psl: xxi, 1]; Epiphanius [Adv: Haer: Lib: ii Haer: lxix, cap. 61-63]; St. Leo [Sermo lxvii, 7; and lxviii, 1, 2]; St. Hilary [De Trin: Lib: x, cap. 62-71]; St. Ambrose [Com: in Luc: Lib: x, cap. 127]; Peter Lombard [Liber Sent: Book iii, dist. 21, q. 1]; &c.

CHAPTER VII

OUR Lord, then, suffered and died as "The Man;" and this brings us to the wider question of the Death upon the Cross as a whole, and to the supreme mystery of the Atonement that underlay that Death; a mystery that can be apprehended in two opposite, and yet correlated ways: namely either from the side of God, or from the side of man.

Taking the latter point of view first, we may say that it was the completeness of our Lord's Incarnation—the perfectness of His humanity—that caused His death. For He was the Holy and True in a world of evil and wrong; and because of this—because of the hatred that evil ever bears to good, and because He fought bravely against the wrong, and by seeking to lead men back to holiness and to God, disturbed the "vested interests" of sin—because of this, I say, He was hunted to His death by the malice of evil men.

And so too will we, if we endeavor to follow in His footsteps, and like Him, to fight against evil and wrong, draw down upon ourselves the bitter hatred of wicked doers; for the betterment of mankind in righteousness and holiness can only be purchased at the cost to the champion of ignominy and suffering, and possibly even of death.

It was, then, because, of the "fall," and the sins of men, that the Primal and Perfect Adam, Incarnate among men, became also the "Man of Sorrows"—the Sufferer of Calvary;—and the prophetic Greek sage read truly the hearts of men, when he said that the perfect man would even be crucified.[95]

Passing on, now, to the first mentioned aspect of the Atonement, namely that of its relation toward God, we may say that while there undoubtedly is this aspect of the death of Christ; and while it must, moreover, be, of necessity, the supreme one; yet nevertheless it must also be, by its very nature, something that we are unable to fully comprehend. For inasmuch as it is an *unique* work—the sole thing of its kind,—it is certainly out of all relation and comparison; and must therefore, in the nature of things, be unknown and unknowable.

And even yet further; in so for as it is an Atonement offered to *God*, it is, manifestly, not to be comprehended, in its fullness, by any but Him; and can even be apprehended by us, only so far as it may practically affect us; and therefore only in a dim and very imperfect way.

---

(95) Vide Plato ["Republic." Book ii, speech of Glaucon to Socrates.] "The just man will be scourged, racked, bound—will have his eyes burnt out; and at last, after suffering every kind of evil, he will be crucified" [or "impaled."]

But yet that there *is* this supreme aspect of the Death upon Calvary—that it *was* an Atonement, offered to God for us—is, I think, evident from the following lines of thought.

In the first place, we have the clear and categorical statements of the Apostles and Evangelists,[96] and even of our Lord Himself[97] to that effect; no one, in fact, who has at all studied the New Testament, can deny that this redemption wrought by Christ is the very heart of its teachings; and is only second in importance to the prime verity of all, namely the Incarnation itself.

Then, in addition, we have the closely connected argument, derived from those prophetic foreshadowings, spoken, or acted—in word, or in type,—that were so abundant under the Old Covenant. For such, and such only, can be the meaning of the various prophecies of Messiah's death;[98] and such, again, is the evident teachings of the ritual sacrifices—those strangely vivid prophetic types—that were so prominent and all important under the Patriarchal, and Jewish Dispensations.

And finally, we have the fact that such an Atonement gives us the only adequate ultimate reason for the Crucifixion of our Lord. For although the malice of evil men was quite capable of compassing that death, and in truth, as I have shown, was its human cause and aspect, yet nevertheless the fact remains that our Lord deliberately exposed Himself to the gratification of that hatred, set His face towards Jerusalem, and suffered Himself to be taken. For surely at any moment, previous to His arrest in the Garden, He could easily have escaped their clutches: and that He refused to do so, but drank to its dregs His cup of suffering, was simply and solely because He would not put that cup aside. It must, then, I think, be allowed that He willingly laid down His Life (St. John, x, 17,18); and that, as He Himself said (St. John, x, 11), to atone for the sins of His people.

Such, then, is the Divine aspect of the death of our Lord upon Calvary: but yet we must, in no case, fall into the terrible error of speaking of that Atonement as if it were the placation of an angry God, by One of a different nature. Ignorant schismatics, whose only apparent commission to preach and explain the Faith lies in their own conceit and selfwill, have too often given occasion for blasphemy by expounding the Atonement as if it were the act of an angry God the Father, unjustly smiting an innocent God the Son; and the "justice, not love" of the Father is sharply contrasted with the "love, not justice" of the Son; as if, forsooth, true justice and true love were ever disunited!

Such an awful heresy, I need scarcely point out, is not only utterly incompatible with the Catholic doctrine of the Trinity,

---

(96) St. John xi, 51, 52; Rom: iii, 25; v, 6; II Cor: v, 18, 19; Heb: ix, 28; I Peter i, 19; ii, 24; I St. John ii, 2; Rev: i, 5; &c.
(97) St. Matt: xx, 28; xxvi, 28; &c.
(98) Gen: iii, 15; Isaiah liii; Daniel ix, 26.

but is also plainly contradicted by the whole of the teaching of the New Testament, and of the Church.

For God the Father, equally with the Son, and Holy Spirit, is *not* a morose and fearful Baal, to be placated by suffering and wrong; but is, on the contrary, the *loving Father of all.* Who willeth the salvation of *every* man from that hideous disease of sin, which alone is the true giver of damnation to our race. He, then, "so loved the world, that He gave His only begotten Son" (St. John, iii, 16); and because He "was in Christ, reconciling the world unto Himself" (II Corin: v, 19), He thereby "commendeth His love toward us" (Rom: v, 8; vide also Eph: ii, 4, 5, etc.).

How far that atoning death of Christ was a necessity in the nature of things it is, of course, impossible for us to comprehend; inasmuch as that lies, as I have already stated, among the incomprehensible prime verities of God. But yet that necessity can possibly be, in some small measure, apprehended, if we will but realise that, even in human affairs, the loving parent cannot, for very love, pass over, unnoticed and unpunished, a serious and growing viciousness in a child; and that not less for the sake of the erring one, than for the protection, and guidance, of his innocent brothers and sisters.

For sin and vice are, not so much unlawful acts, as evidences of a diseased state of the soul—a blasting, and cankering destruction of the primary "image" of God;—inasmuch as a soul, lost and damned by a "habitual" preference for evil, has certainly lost, not only its primary love for holiness and truth, but also, with that love, even the Logos-like faculty of reason; for sin and wrong are, by their very nature, unreasonable, and exclusive of all Right Reason, and Truth.[100]

It follows, therefore, that the punishment—even the drastic punishment—of a sinner, during his growth towards that terrible "habitual sinfulness," is, in no sense, cruel or vindictive; but is, on the contrary, strictly remedial in its character; and therefore merciful and loving, and worthy of the Great Father of all.

God, then, because He is Loving and Merciful, no less than because He is Holy, cannot but abhor, and punish sin; and that, too, not merely for the protection and guidance of His unfallen creatures, but even for the sake of sinful man himself.

He came, therefore, to redeem His people *from* their sins—not *in* them;—for the company of the pure and holy would be no heaven to an impure man; but, on the contrary, a state of intolerable anguish; and it would not be until such a man was redeemed from his sin, and made pure and holy, and that, too, only

---

(99) Compare pp. 41 et seq., and note 69, and what is there said concerning "habit."
(100) Vide the Essay on "the Essential Nature of Sin;" and also compare the wise Arabic proverb that "the most grievous evil that can befall a sinner is to *be* a sinner;" and again, the saying " ἡ δὲ κακὴ βουλὴ τῷ βουλεύσαντι κακίστη."

with his own acquiescence,[101] but that he would be, not merely *fit*, but *able* to enjoy the Beatific Vision of his God.

Sin, then, must not only be marked by God's abhorence and condemnation, but man must be purified from it; and both these conditions we find fulfilled in the awful tragedy of the Cross; so that men have ever there seen both God's love to the sinner, and His abhorrence of sin; and have thereby been moved, as nothing else could move them, to loathe and forsake that sin, and to enlist under the banner of the Crucified: as our Lord Himself, then, said "I, if I be lifted up, will draw all men unto Me."

We come, therefore, to our God, not only as His creatures, or even as children formed in the "image" of the Son, but also as redeemed ones, bearing in our hands the Sacrificial Blood; for by that right, and that right alone, have we "access to the holiest;" and are made, in short, One Mystical Body with our Great High Priest and Head.

Christ, then, as the "Son of Man," was our Sacrifice and Atonement; and this brings me to the consideration of an obscure, and yet most fruitful line of thought, namely the question in what sense, and in what degree, may we, as "members incorporate in Him," be truly said to be partakers in "the fellowship of His sufferings?"

Now it is sometimes stated (although not by Catholic theologians), as a self evident fact, that as Christ's "merit" is infinite, the "merit" of His Passion is infinite also; and as such, cannot be affected by, or have any relation to, any sufferings that we may endure; or in other words, that we of His Body—the Church,—having been redeemed from sin, have no further part or lot in the matter; our connection with the Atonement wrought for sinners being, purely and solely, passive in its character.

Yet surely our Lord suffered on the Cross, not as Very and Infinite God, but as very and finite *man:* and therefore the "merit" of His Passion was finite also, and atoned for the sins of a finite race: Christ, in short, I repeat, suffered, not apart from man, but *as Man*—as the Great Head of our race;—and we, therefore, as "members incorporate in Him," have our part in the work, and must carry our portion of the Cross—bear our share of the sufferings and woe of the world, and give our quota of painful toil towards the redemption of mankind.

This certainly appears to be the meaning, not only of that expression in Philippians iv, 10, already quoted, namely "the fellowship of His sufferings," but also of those words of St. Paul in Colossians i. 24, bidding us to "fill up that which is behind in the afflictions of Christ."[102]

---

(101) Vide what is said on pp. 41 et seq. on the necessity of freedom to holiness: compare also note 72.
(102) Vide also Rom: viii, 17; II Cor: i, 5, 7; iv, 10; II St. Tim: ii, 12; I St. Peter iv, 13; v. 10; &c.

But yet, of course, it is not, in any sense, true that the redemption wrought by our Lord upon Calvary lacked aught of completeness; such an idea would, plainly, be repulsive to every Christian sentiment, and would even be formally heretical.

Nevertheless it is, I think, evidently true that, in our Lord's Atonement, He presented, not only His own individual humanity, but also that of His whole Mystical Body yet to be; and just as all the aspirations and capabilities of humanity were summed up in the Incarnation; so also were all its sufferings and agonies over sin gathered in one on the Cross.[103]

It follows, then, that every saint, every martyr, aye! and every sincere member of Christ's Church, is, in some real sense, a partaker in the fellowship of those sufferings; so that even in this redeeming aspect of our Lord's humanity may it be said that He is, in some measure, our "Example."

And perhaps also, in this connection, should be noted the purifying effect upon the soul of sorrow and suffering; for this, together with the "corporate" nature of our Lord's death, upon which I am insisting, may possibly throw some light upon the Sacrificial aspect of His Atonement.

Christ, then, as our High Priest, and that, not merely by right of His Logos Mediatorship, but also, and especially, by reason of His primary Archetypal likeness to, and later Incarnation in, man, as our High Priest, I say, and the great Head of our race, offered up to God the Atonement for sin; and thereby redeemed us by His own blood. And having finished this work, He died the natural death of a man, and descended[104] into the "Hell" or "Hades" of the dead, thus fulfilling the whole experience of man.

And this estate of the dead is, evidently, no inconsiderable portion of our existence; for it will last from death until the Resurrection Day; when, with the bodies our God shall give us, we will wake to active life once more.

But yet this season in "Hell" must not be imagined simply as a time of mere stupor and total unconsciousness; and that for the principal reason that our Lord—our Archetypal "Example,"—during His sojourn in that "Hell" as a man, was not, in His humanity, so unconscious and inactive; but on the contrary, preached to those "spirits in prison" the redemption He had made (I Peter, iii, 19; iv, 6).

---

(103) Vide St. Augustine [Epist: cxl, cap. vi, § 18]. "Ecclesia in illo patiebatur, quando pro Ecclesia patiebatur. Nam sicut audivimus Ecclesia vocem in Christo patientis 'Deus! Deus Meus! quare Me dereliquisti?'" * * * [Cap. xi, § 20], "sed procul dubio non in illis vocibus eramus, et Caput pro suo corpore loquebatur." * * * [Cap xiii, § 33.] "Clamat ergo martyris anima transfigurata in Christo." St. Leo [Sermo lxix, and lxx]; St. Thomas Aquinas [Exp: in Davidem, Psl: xxii]; &c.

See also, what is said on p. 57, and in note 94 concerning the representative nature of our Lord's cry upon the cross.

And furthermore, as I may here remark, this consideration will also show us the utter falsity of those highly artificial and unreal "forensic" theories of the Atonement, put forth by Calvinistic and Lutheran teachers.

(104) i. e. in His human "anima"—or "mind," and "vital life"—; *not* in His Godhead; which, because Omnipresent, cannot partake of any change of locality. See, similarly, note 119 on the "Ascension."

And yet, on the other hand, it cannot be a time of such activity and fullness of life as we now enjoy, with our present body; and will enjoy hereafter, with our "resurrection body;" and that for the following reasons: in the first place, we, evidently, now have this fullness of life because, and only because, our body, with its Cosmos of sensational nerves receiving impressons from, and motor nerves conveying activities to our environment—the material world around us,—places us in active relation to that world; and thus enables us to have active life: and in the second place, unless a material body were so necessary for the full exercise of the powers of our "Ego"—or in other words, unless a body were such a necessary medium and instrument of the "Egoistic" Spirit, and not such a mere prison house to, and clog upon, the faculties of that Spirit, as Dualistic, or quasi-dualistic thinkers falsely suppose[105]—unless, I say, the material body were such a necessary instrument, there would obviously be neither meaning to, nor fitness in, a resurrection body for the redeemed soul.[106]

The body, then, evidently is, and must be, a necessity for the exercise of the full activities of the "Ego;" and when, therefore, from various causes, the lesion of death occurs, we thereby become "naked" and "unclothed," and are reduced to a state of proportionate helplessness; and perforce, must lie in "Hell," until we are once more "clothed upon" with our "spiritual"[107] body on the Resurrection Morn.

Perhaps, then, our existence in that estate of the dead may best be pictured, not as a stupor of unconsciousness, as I have already remarked, but rather as partaking of the nature of a gentle and timeless dream; in which our relations will be principally with the Immanent and Inspiring Logos; Who there, as here, will ever be giving us being; and only indirectly (so to speak), and through Him, with our fellow creatures in "Hell."

From this, then, it follows that our happiness, or misery, during this season in "Hades," will depend, solely and entirely, upon this relation of ours with the Logos, or in other words, upon our capacity for enjoying a measure of the "Vision" of our Lord.

Thus, to illustrate, we can well believe that those blessed ones who know, and perfectly love Him, even now, will enjoy, in that "Vision," all the bliss possible to a being, who is yet debarred from active and perfect life, by reason of the lack of a body: on the other hand, those of us who die, full of manifold faults and imperfections, and yet sincerely and truly loving our Lord, will surely, by that "Vision," be filled with mingled bliss and loving remorse for our many shortcomings and infirmities; a remorse that

---

(105) On this point, and this whole discussion on the inter-relations of "body" and "spirit," see the Essays on "The Essential Nature of Sin," and on "Spirit and Matter."
(106) Which body, as a matter of fact, is, as we know, denied by all the dualistic and quasi-dualistic "Spiritualizers;" vide, again the Essay on "The Essential Nature of Sin."
(107) Vide what is said, further on, concerning this "spiritual" body.

will burn away those infirmities, as nothing else could do, and purify us in its fierce, yet cleansing flame.

And yet again; those souls who have, until this season, been ignorant of their God, or seen Him, at the best, but dimly through their heathen faiths, and yet, despite of this, have followed and obeyed, as best they could, His guidings and "enlightenings" of their minds, those souls, I say, will doubtless, in that "Vision," at last receive the Full Light, hear His Gospel, and know Him as their Lord.[108]

While, finally, those wicked ones who, in this life, have chosen evil for their guide, and have thereby lost their Logos-imaged manhood, and become transmuted into fiends, what can such unhappy ones experience in this relation, but solitude, agony, and woe? And in this instance, alas! it will not be, as in the case of the imperfect, yet sincere Christian, a remedial suffering, springing from remorseful love, and purifying the nature, even as the silver is purified in the fire; but will rather be the hopeless, and self inflicted tortures of a hateful nature, eating out its own heart with malice and hatred to all around.

Such, then, I think, is the clearest conception that we can form of our existence as unclothed spirits in "Hades," or "Hell:"[109] and yet, as it may be remarked, this picture, and especially what I have said concerning our activities, although probable in many ways, is yet, at the last analysis, but speculative, or at least inductive, and therefore not absolutely certain; all that we, as Catholic theologians, can surely say is that there is this "Hell"—this estate of the disembodied dead;—and that our Lord, in taking our true nature upon Him, and fulfilling our whole existence,

---

(108) Vide 1 St. Peter iii, 19, 20; conf: also Acts x, 34, 35; and our Lord's judgment of the "nations" [i. e. the *heathen*] in St. Matt: xxv, 31-46. In this category, also, evidently belong unbaptised infants.

(109) Compare, on all the foregoing discussion, St. Luke xvi, 22-31; xxiii, 43; II Cor: v. 1-8; Philip: ii, 23; Heb: xii, 23; I St. Peter iii, 19. 20; Rev vi, 9-11. Also Hermas [Lib: iii. Simil: 9, § 16]; St. Clemens Alex: [Strom: Lib: vi, cap. 6]; St. Irenaeus ["Adv: Haer:" Lib: ii, cap. 33, 34, and v, cap. 31]; Tertullian ["De Anima" cap. 53-58]; Lactantius [Inst: Div: Lib: vii, cap. 9, et seq.]; St. Hilary [Exp: in Psl: cxx, § 16; and cxxxviii, § 22]; St. Gregory Nazianzen [Orat: xxxix, § 19; and xl, § 16]; St. Ambrose [De Bono Mortis, cap. 10]; St. Augustine ["Enchir:" cap. 69, and 109; "De Civitate Dei, xxi, 13]; St. Gregory the Great [Dial: iv]; St. Thomas Aquinas [Sum: Theo: Pars iii, qq. lxix and lxx], &c.

It is, probably, unnecessary to here remark that in all the previous discussion of the estate of the disembodied dead, "Hell" is *not* used in the commonly understood sense of "Gehenna"—i. e. the *final* estate, or place of the damned,—but only in the sense implied in the Creed, and as equivalent to the "Hades" of the New Testament and the "Sheol" of the Old.

And furthermore: on this point the whole Catholic Church is in actual and real [although not *nominal*] agreement; for while Anglicans generally speak of this estate as "Hades," or "Hell" [for all souls in general], and "Paradise" [for the blessed dead, in particular], Roman Catholics distinguish the various estates as "Purgatory" [for imperfect Christians], "Heaven" [for the perfected saints: also used for the estate of *final* and *post-resurrection* glory, thus lying open to the danger of a confusion in terminology], and "Hell" [for the "habitually 'evil; again also used for the *final* estate of the damned, with a resultant ambiguity]; "Limbus Patrum," "Puerorum," &c. Greek Catholics, on the other hand, speak of but two estates, "Heaven" [by which is meant as in the Roman Church, both the final and eternal estate of the redeemed, and also their present and temporal estate in "Paradise"], and "Hell" [under which term is included all "Hades, *except* "Paradise;" and also the final and eternal estate of the lost.] While, therefore, there is some confusion of *terms*, yet the common agreement in *meaning* is, I think, substantial.

could not but pass through that season in "Hell;" and thus unify Himself with that vast army of the dead.

And during this descent into "Hell" the Hypostatic Union was still complete; for (as has been already noted on p. 24) He, the Essentially Omnipresent Logos, ever Immanent in His Universe, and Eternally in the Bosom of the Father, was evidently present in, and manifested by His human soul in Hell, as He was also present in, and (to its measure) manifested by His human body in the tomb.[110]

This latter presence of our Lord, that namely with His human body in the grave, is evident, I think, not only from His Essential Omnipresence, but also from the following considerations. If that body had been forsaken in death by the Divine Immanence, as it was by our Lord's human life, then the Catholic formula of "never to be divided" would, clearly, be contradicted: and even furthermore the Resurrection, in such a case, would have been, not simply even a *re-Incarnation*, but rather a Nestorian *re-possession*. This is plainly untenable; and we must, therefore, recognise the Hypostatic Union as unimpaired; so that, even in death, there was no element of His humanity that, for one single instant, existed apart from Him.

But having fulfilled this portion of our existence, and "tasted death for every man," He rose again the third day from the dead;[111] and taking His body from the grave (in which, as I have stated, He never had ceased to be present) He revivified and transformed it, in some subtle way, into the "Resurrection" or "spiritual" body; called "spiritual," not because it is subjective and illusionary, nor even because it is non-material, but simply and solely because it is completely under the sway of the spiritual faculties.[112]

---

(110) Vide St. Athanasius ["De Incar: contra Apoll:" Lib: ii, § 14.] "μήτε τῆς Θεότητος τοῦ σώματος ἐν τῷ τάφῳ ἀπολιμπανομ νκς, μήτε τῆς ψυχῆς ἐν τῷ ᾅδῃ χωριζομένης;" and [De Sal: Adv: J. C., Lib: i, pp. 645, 646.] "ὥστε οὐκ ἄνθρωπος Θεὸν ἐχωρίζετο, ὅτε Θεὸς πρὸς ἄνθρωπον ἐγκατάλειψιν διηγεῖτο οὔτε ἡ νέκρωσις ἀποχώρησις Θεοῦ, ἢ ἀπὸ σώματος ἦν μετάστασις, ἀλλὰ ψυχῆς ἀπὸ σώματος χωρισμός;" St. Augustine [De Fide et Symbolo. Lib: iii, cap. 7.] "Totus Filius apud Patrem, totus in coelo totus in terra. totus in utero Virginis, totus in cruce, totus in inferno, totus in paradiso quo latronem introduxit;" and [Tract: in Joan:" 47. § 9]; St. Leo [Sermo lxxi, 2.] "Quoniam Deitas quae ab utraque suscepti hominis substantia non recessit, quod potestate divisit, potestate conjunxit." St. John Damascene [De Fide Orth: Lib: iii, cap. 27; and Lib: iv. cap. 1]; Peter Lombard [Liber Sent: Book iii. dist: 22, q. 2.] "Et utique totus eodem tempore erat in inferno, in coelo totus, ubique totus." and St. Thomas Aquinas [Sum: Theo: Pars iii. Q. lii, art. 3.] "Totus Christus fuit in sepulchro, quia tota Persona fuit ibi per corpus sibi unitum; et similiter totus fuit in inferno, quia tota Persona Christi fuit ibi ratione animae sibi unitae: totus etiam Christus tunc erat ubique, ratione Divinae Naturae." Vide, also, p. 24 and note 22.

(111) The consideration of the various evidences for the *fact* of the Resurrection of our Lord, is evidently outside of the scope of this present treatise; for my design here is merely to expound and unfold, as far as may be, the substance, and bearing of the Catholic doctrine of the Incarnation. I must, therefore, reserve for another occasion the examination of the evidences in favour of the Resurrection; and the rebuttal of the various sceptical theories—namely, that it was a mere revival from a swoon, or was a myth, or an illusion. &c.—by which some have endeavoured to explain it away.

(112) Vide St. Thomas Aquinas [Sum: Theo: Pars iii, Q liv art 1, ad. 2.] "Haec est autem dispositio corporis gloriosi, ut sit spirituale, id est subjectum spiritui ut Apostolus dicit [I Cor: xv.] Ad hoc autem quod sit omnino corpus subjectum Spiritui, re-

Our Lord's resurrection body, in short, was, in no sense, an unique and miraculous one; but was, on the contrary, an entirely natural one; and proper to the resurrection man."[113] For just as the body of His humiliation, wherein He suffered, and was crucified, was no mere Doketic apparition, but a real human body, that could, and did actually, hunger, and become weary, and feel pain, so too was His resurrection body, simply and solely, that natural human body, raised from the grave, and "glorified"—even "sublimated," if we may use the term—by His Spirit, as our bodies shall be by our spirits; and thus made a "spiritual" body, and agreeable to its new conditions and environments.

That this is true—that Christ's risen body is simply the body proper to the risen man,—is evident, I think, from the following considerations. In the first place, such is the plain statement of St. Paul, both in his Epistle to the Philippians (iii, 21), and especially in his well known argument for the resurrection in I Corinth. xv, where he uses the fact of our Lord's Resurrection as conclusively showing that we too shall be raised.

And, in the second place, if Christ be not our "Example," here as elsewhere in His Incarnate Life, it is hard to see what can be the meaning and teaching of His Resurrection; for He evidently rose again, as He had lived and died, solely as the Incarnate One; or in other words, not in His Divine and non-Incarnate Estate as Very God, but in His human and Incarnate Estate as Very Man. This being so, then our Lord's resurrection body is clearly an "example" of what ours shall be, when we rise from the dead, re-create our bodies around our "hypostatic Ego," and thus "awake in His likeness."

This "spiritual" body to be is, no doubt, largely incomprehensible to us now; for it is, in many respects, outside of the categories of our present experience and knowledge: but yet we may possibly form some slight conception of it by considering that, even now, our bodies are sustained, and, to a large extent, moulded by, our hypostatic and creative "Ego;" and are thereby enabled to more or less efficiently meet and conquer those constant changes of environment that constitute "life."

But sin, by introducing discordances, has both marred the perfection of our nature, and also introduced conflicting "environments"—has, in short, made many things "natural" and easy to one part of our nature, that are, at the same time, "unnatural," abhorent, and destructive to another part;[114] and thus, as I have

---

quiritur quod omnis actio corporis subdatur spiritus voluntati;" also St. Augustine [De Fide et Symbolo, cap. vi, § 13.] &c.

(113) Vide St. Thomas Aquinas [Sum: Theo: Pars iii, Q. liv. art. 1, ad. 1.] "Ad primum ergo dicendum quod Corpus Christi post resurrectionem non ex miraculo, sed ex conditione gloriae, &c."

(114) Thus, to take an instance, a dweller in one of our "slums" has "environments" of—or "correspondences" with—(1) the laws of God, and of right, (2) the laws of his nature, and its appetites—inherited, or acquired,—(3) the laws of the land, and of "society" as a whole, and finally, (4) the "common law," or usages of his particular "society." Now all these "laws" are, more or less, interconflicting and opposite; and

stated, has introduced discordances that ultimately issue in death.

But in the resurrection life, our body, we believe, will be a "spiritual" one; and as such, entirely under the sway of our "Ego;" which "Ego," again, will be pure and holy, and without any conflicting appetites; so that whatever we may naturally desire, we may lawfully and rightly do. When, therefore, we pass into the "heavenly mansions," we will be in perfect agreement with our God; and in the enjoyment of the Beatific Vision, will be also in harmony with all our "environment"—with our own nature, with the angelic host, and with our redeemed brethren:—so that our souls will be no more torn by conflicting emotions, or desires; but in that knowledge of our God, will have perfect satisfaction and eternal life; for our correspondences with our environment will ever be perfect."[a]

Such, then, so far as we can imagine it, will be our resurrection state; and of this estate we have, as I have just said, an example in our risen Lord. For His body was, evidently, a "spiritual" one; and as such, given whatever form His creative "Ego" might will; He therefore could appear (St. Luke, xxiv, 36; St. John, xx, 19 and 26), and disappear from sight (St. Luke, xxiv, 31); and could even, on occasions, present another appearance to His disciples (St. Mark, xvi, 12; St. Luke, xxiv, 16 and 31; St. John, xxi, 4). With reference to this latter point we may note that, even in this present life, the "Ego" has great influence on the appearance of the outer man; a brutal countenance bespeaks a brutal soul, and "vice versa;" and again, our loves, our hates, our fears, and our joys are all reflected in our visage; and finally, if a refined and good man should fall into sin, and commit a brutal act, his whole appearance is thereby changed, and that to a very startling degree. Truly, therefore, even in this life, as I have said, the "Ego" moulds the body; and what bounds, then, can we put to the changes that may be wrought by it in the resurrection life?

A rather difficult minor point, in connection with the "spiritual" body lies in the *eating* by our Lord on several occasions preceding His Ascension (St. Luke, xxiv, 43; St. John, xxi, 13). Possibly we may explain this by saying that inasmuch as the resurrection body, both in our Lord's case, and in ours, consists of material particles"[b](although those particles are so entirely under the sway of the spiritual faculties as to deserve the name of a

---

whatever set he obeys, he thereby transgresses, and is punished by the other "correspondences;" his life, therefore, must ever be a more or less unhappy one.

(115) Compare the saving of Herbert Spencer, "perfect correspondence would be perfect life. Were there no changes in the environment, but such as the organism had adopted changes to meet, and were it never to fail in the efficiency with which it meet them, there would be *eternal existence*, and *universal knowledge*." Does not all this exactly agree with our Lord's words "This is *life eternal*, that they might know Thee, the only true God, and Jesus Christ, Whom Thou hast sent" [St. John xvii. 3].

(116) And that because it is a *body*; vide what is said on pp. 62 and 63 as to the disembodied dead; and also the Essay on "Spirit and Matter."

"spiritual" body), yet, I say, inasmuch as that body consists of material particles, it must needs be subject to friction and wear, and therefore stand in need of constant renewal. For "life," in its very nature, consists, not in changelessness (which would rather be death), but in constant movement; and the eternal life, therefore, of the body will not consist in an eternal sameness; but will rather, as I have stated, be an eternally perfect meeting of the constantly changing environment.

If this be true, then we may possibly conceive how our Lord, in order to reassure His disciples of His material reality (St. Luke, xxiv, 39), might, on a few occasions, take from common food those new particles required for the renewal of His body, that He ordinarily would take directly from the surrounding elements. But this is an obscure speculation; and must, therefore, be taken by the reader for what it is worth.

Another very curious question, and one, I think, that has never been previously raised, concerns the nature of our Lord's resurrection vesture.

That He was so vested is, certainly, evident to anyone who reads the account of His appearances to His disciples: and furthermore; as He did not always present the same appearance, it is, presumably, but reasonable to conclude that His vesture on each of those occasions—say, for instance, on Easter morning, on the road to Emmaus, or at the Galilean lake—was also different: and, yet again, we may notice the similar vestments of the angels [e. g. St. Matt., xxviii, 3; St. Mark, xvi, 5; St. Luke, xiv, 4; St. John, xx, 12, etc.], and of the redeemed ones in bliss [Rev., vii, 9].

And yet these garments, both in our Blessed Lord's case, and in our own, cannot well be thought of as things separate from, external, and foreign to the "resurrection body,"—cannot, in other words, hold to it such a mere extraneous relation as that now existing between our present body and its garments,—inasmuch as, in such a case, we would have to make the rather improbable hypothesis of a restoration, or recreation, of our human fabrics and fashions!

The solution of the enigma seems, to me, to be, perhaps, as follows: the resurrection body, as I have already remarked [vide pp. 66, 67][117] will not be something that is external to us, and separately created, and into which we are put; but will, on the contrary, be rather the creation, and perfect expression of our "hypostatic" Ego—the "phenomenon," in other words, of that "noumenon." In such a case, then, it is, I believe, quite conceivable that the Ego, in "projecting around itself" [so to speak], as its "expression," a body, should also "project," or "express" any vestings of that body that it might will to create.

This, of course, is merely given as a hypothesis; but yet it

---

(117) Vide also the Essay on "Spirit and Matter."

seems to me to be also one that is perfectly feasible and defensible.

There is yet one final point on which it may be well to touch: when we receive our resurrection bodies, and attain unto the heaven of God, our existence, as of our bodies, so of our spirits, will not, as I have previously stated, be an eternal sameness; but will doubtless be rather a growth from glory unto ever higher glories—a constant advance into ever increasing knowledge and perfection. Yet such a growth in perfection cannot, I think, be truly predicated of the Human Nature of our Lord: for although His Humanity is certainly a true one, and is exactly akin to our own in that it is given entire being by, and is a faithful reflection of, the hypostatic "Ego," or "Spirit," yet it widely differs in this one respect; with us, in heaven, that creative "Ego" will still be finite; and, therefore, will be capable, as I have stated, of a constant development in knowledge and perfection; which development will constitute its "life." But in His case, there will be no such capacity for development; for His Hypostatic "Ego" is the Infinite, Omniscient, and All Perfect Logos, in Whom any growth, or increase is unthinkable; while His humanity—mental life, bodily life, and body—although certainly essentially finite, and even furthermore, once the subject of such "growth" (vide pp. 37 and 38), is yet now, it seems to me, fully "grown" in all respects, and completely "habituated" to His Will (vide p. 44 et seq.); it, therefore, can only now "grow" in compliance with an equal development in that Will, or Hypostatic "Ego;" and any such development, as I have just shown, is impossible to Him.[18]

It follows, then, I think, that our Lord's glorified humanity, although certainly kindred in all other respects to our own, will yet not, like ours, grow from glory unto glory; but will rather be the Eternally Perfect Ideal, to Which we will ever be attaining.

(1:8) But therefore, also, on the other hand, possible to us; for while our "spiritual body" will, as I have previously stated, like His, be in perfect agreement with our perfect and redeemed "Ego;" and therefore be "perfect" of its kind; yet inasmuch as that "Ego," being finite, as well as perfect, can, and must develop in perfection, so also must the "spiritual body" it gives being to, develop with it to an equal degree.

CHAPTER X

OUR Lord, then, on that first Easter morning, rose from the dead, and manifested forth this ideal humanity—body, mind, and "Ego"—of the resurrection life; and having done so, spent forty days on earth among His disciples, before His Ascension into Heaven: this, as we are plainly told (Acts i, 3), was for the sake of confirming their faith, and instructing them in the things pertaining to the Kingdom of God.

But having fulfilled this work, He then Ascended into Heaven, there to be our Great High Priest before the Throne of God.[119]

And this office He is able to fulfill because, and only because, He—the Mediating Logos—has become also the "Son of Man"—has, in other words, as I have shown in this treatise, taken our nature truly upon Him, has suffered, and been tempted, like ourselves, and finally has died for us upon the Cross, passed through "Hell," and risen again from the tomb. Had He not have been so Incarnate, and so partaken of our griefs, He might, no doubt, have been our "King," our "Lord," even our "Prophet;" but He could hardly have been our "Priest;" for the prime and essential note of priesthood is, not superiority, or even holiness [although this, too, is necessary],[120] but likeness and sympathy. This likeness, then, and sympathy He has acquired by His Incarnation and life; and is, therefore, as our Brother, our Merciful and Faithful High Priest before the Throne on High.

It is, again, by reason of this assumption of our nature by our Lord, that we, as His fellow men and brethren, are able to become "members incorporate in Him;" and therefore, also, be partakers in His Priesthood. For all the faithful, in their several "orders" as "Bishops," "Priests," "Deacons," or "Laymen" of His Church, are His commissioned and corporate representatives — His "priests"—to the world, and to God; and, as such, preach, on the one hand, His Gospel to mankind; and on the other, offer up to God the Eucharistic Sacrifice of His Passion. And this, I repeat, is because, and only because, He has first become One with us; and is, by His Incarnation, our Elder Brother and Head.

---

(119) Ascended, *not* in His *Omnipresent* Estate as the Logos [concerning Whom any transmission, or transference through space is, manifestly, incredible], but in His *finite* Estate, as Incarnate, and manifest to man.

Vide St. Thomas Aquinas [Sum: Theo: Pars iii, Q. lvii, art. 2]. "Ascendit Christus in coelum, non secundum Divinam Naturam, quae nunquam coelum deseruit, sed secundum quod homo virtute Divinitatis penetravit coelos."

See also note 104 on the "descent" of our Lord into "Hell;" and compare the note at the end of this treatise on "the Local Manifestation."

(120) Vide what is said upon the necessity of sinlessness to perfect sympathy [and consequently, to priesthood] at the close of the Essay on "the Essential Nature of Sin."

And so, again, is the Holy Ghost—the Lord and Giver of life—given by our Lord to His Church, to be her Vivifying and Guiding Soul, simply and solely, because of this incorporate relation to Himself. For the Holy Spirit, by His Essence, Eternally Proceedeth from the Father, through the Son; and is, therefore, necessarily given by the Son to those whom He has made One with Himself by means of His Incarnation and Redemption.

It, therefore, evidently follows that, as I have stated at the beginning of this treatise, the Incarnation is the central and vital fact of Christianity, and the plenary well spring of all its teachings, and Sacramental grace; in that from it depends all the Church's Gospel and Theology, all her Sacraments and ritual, all her Priesthood and Mission, even her very existence itself, and the Immanent Life she ever derives from the Holy Spirit of God.

This being the case, it may be well to theoretically inquire if the Incarnation would not have taken place, even if man had not fallen; or in other words, if the reason for the Incarnation does not lie deep in humanity itself, the effect of the "Fall" and of sin being, not to cause, but rather to modify that "Intention of Creation;" and turn it, for a season, into a time of suffering and anguish —making the Incarnation, in short, become also the Atonement.

The reasons for thinking this probably are very weighty, and may be briefly summed up as follows. If it be supposed that the "Fall" was really an essential to the Incarnation, then we should at once be confronted with the fact that, in such a case, man, by becoming a sinner, has attained to blessings and favors—even to the supreme knowledge of, and union with His God—that He might never have hoped for had he remained obedient! Such an idea is surely repugnant to our sense of the fitness of things; "o felix culpa!"[121] is certainly not the true characterisation of disobedience and wrong.

And secondly, we have the very strong argument that, inasmuch as our Lord is the Primal and Archetypal Adam, in Whose "image" man had first been made (vide pp. 25 et seq.), man, therefore, by the very constitution of his being and nature, called for such an assimilation to his God as was wrought in the Incarnation; which assimilation, as I have shown (p. 2 et seq.), he longs for, and is unsatisfied until he attains; and finally, which having attained, he is capable of both appreciating and receiving.

Sin and the "Fall," on the other hand, so far from helping this "assimilation," have, on the contrary, greatly hindered and retarded it; and by blurring and injuring the Divine "Image" in our nature, have rendered the work of the Incarnate One, if possibly (humanly speaking) "more necessary;" certainly also more painful and difficult.

---

(121) As Richard de S. Victor exclaimed [De Verbo Incar: cap. 3].

In short, we may say that the benefits of the Incarnation are neither summed up by, and commensurate with, nor exhausted by the Atonement, and man's redemption from sin. For although the assumption of our nature by our God is certainly the way we are, and apparently the only way we could be, redeemed from our sin, and made holy and righteous, yet this is true because, and only because, we are, first and foremost, drawn thereby into union with our God; our purification being, in short, not a precedent, but a consequence of thus being made One with Him.[122] The Incarnation, then, in brief, is the major and primary fact; and as such, must evidently include the Atonement, as it does all else in Christianity; and not "vice versa;" so that we may well conclude that even if man had not fallen, the Logos would still have become Incarnate.[123]

Yet another argument in support of this reasoning, and that a most subtle one, lies in the dual character and order of the Eucharistic elements. Our Lord, it will be noticed, first gave His Body for the life of the world, to make us One with Himself (compare St. John, vi, 32-58; and I Corinth., x, 17); and then, and only then, did He give His Atoning Blood, poured out for the remission of sins (St. Matt., xxvi, 28). This is, I repeat, a most subtle argument; and yet certainly one that powerfully reinforces the other considerations mentioned.

Continuing this line of thought we may say that, even without the "Fall," there would doubtless have been a "Virgin Birth;" and that both because the Incarnation would still have been a *new beginning* — the coming of the Head of our race;—and also because it would otherwise have been no true "Incarnation" at all, but the mere Nestorian "possession" of a man inspired by God (vide p. 29).

And having become so Incarnate among un-fallen men, while there, obviously, would have been no necessity for, or meaning in His sufferings and Atonement, yet He certainly would still unite us with Himself, possibly even by an Eucharistic rite; and thus, no doubt, have caused us to be transformed, even as He was at His Transfiguration, without passing through the agonies and ignominies of death, into the "Spiritual body" of the Resurrection life (vide pp. 48 and 49).

But yet, of course, all this is mere theoretical speculation; for

---

(122) Popular "revivalism" often forgets this vital fact, when it urges people to *first* "become holy," either by "works," or [more generally] by "faith" [by which term a self excited emotional experience is intended]; and then, having so "become holy," and "experienced religion," to "come to God," and "join the Christian Church." But this erroneous teaching overlooks, as I have said, the fact that, firstly, we cannot, apart from God, make ourselves holy, even by "works," and certainly not by emotion; and secondly, that, as our Lord Himself said, He came, not to call the righteous, but *sinners* to repentance. We come, therefore to Christ, and to His body—the Church,—*not* as self conscious and self sufficient "saints," seeking admission, for the mere purpose of edification, into a "holy club;" but as sinful men—"lost pieces of silver," yet with the image and superscription of the Great King,—coming to Him Who is our Archetypal Brother, Redeemer, and Priest.

(123) Compare the Nicene phrase "for us men, *and* for our salvation," &c.

man having fallen, The Incarnate One became, of necessity, also the "Man of Sorrows"—the Crucified Lamb of God.'[123]

Such, then, is the Church's doctrine of the Incarnation of the Logos; a doctrine that is, as I trust I have shown, perfectly coherent, and self consistent; and in accurate agreement with all the known facts of our Lord's Person and life.

It remains now to be seen if it can be also substantiated by positive arguments; or if, on the other hand, it is a mere fine spun theory, very beautiful, no doubt, and well rounded; but yet with no more solid basis than the poetic imagination.

Of course, as I stated towards the commencement of this treatise (p. 8), a full and detailed examination of the various evidences for the historical facts of Christianity is outside of my present design; which is merely to elucidate and unfold, as far as may be, the Church's doctrine concerning that Incarnation.

But yet, this work having now been accomplished, a brief sketch of some of the arguments in favour of the actual agreement with reality of that doctrine will, I think, both be suitable here, and will also make a fit close to the discussion.

To begin, then, we may say that the very self consistence and coherency of the doctrine is, in itself, no despicable argument; for false or inaccurate theories are, invariably, somewhere, or in some respects, self conflicting and illogical; perfect agreement, both with itself, and its surroundings, belongs only to truth.

But even passing over this consideration, we have the following positive arguments. In the first place, there are, on the one hand, the definite and repeated claims of our Lord to be the Eternal Logos of God, Incarnate among men;[125] and on the other hand, the various circumstances of His life, His teaching, His death, and resurrection. In view, then, of these claims and this life, He must evidently be held to be "aut Deus, aut homo non bonus," alternatives of which we must certainly choose the first.[126] He Who walked those Galilean fields was certainly, if our appreciation of truth can at all be trusted, no deluding, or self deluded imposter; but was what He claimed to be, namely the Incarnate Word, tabernacling among men.

Then a second line of argument consists in that centering in, and preparation for His coming, to which I have already alluded at the beginning of this treatise. For, as I there endeavoured to

---

(124) St. Thomas Aquinas [Sum: Theo: Pars iii, Q. i, art. 3]. it is true, while he grants that "potuisset enim etiam peccato non existente Deus incarnari," yet rather inclines to the opinion that the "fa'l" was a necessary precedent to the Incarnation; and this because the redemption of man is always, in Holy Scripture, linked with that Incarnation.

Yet this reasoning, it seems to me, is not quite to the point; inasmuch as the question is, not what is actually the case *now* [for all grant that, under present conditions, the Incarnation and the Atonement are inseparable], but what, theoretically, *might* have been, *had man not fallen*. Under this latter supposition, the view I have advanced in the text seems, to me, to be impregnable.

(125) Vide St. Matt: xi, 27; xxviii, 19; St. John iii, 13-21; v, 17-47; x, 30; xiv; xv, 26; xvi, 15; xvii, 10; &c.

(126) For a full discussion of this point, I beg to refer to Canon Liddon's Bampton Lectures "On the Divinity of our Lord."

show, both the ideas—the "logoi"—of Nature, and the basic elements of humanity, all proceed from, center in, aspire to, and are only fulfilled in, the Logos; thus giving rise to the thirst of the soul for Him; which thirst, again, can only be satisfied by His revelation to us in His Incarnation.

And even furthermore: humanity, as I pointed out, was not only implicitly, but also explicitly awaiting Him; as the prophesies and foreshadowings in the heathen religions show (vide. pp. 4-5) He was, then, the Ideal of the Ages—the fulfillment and satisfaction of man's fervent desire for God;—and as such, was truly the Logos Incarnate.

And, thirdly, we may continue this line of thought by pointing to all secular history, both before, and since His coming. We date our chronologies "B. C.," and "A. D.;" and this is no mere Christian prejudice, but is amply warranted by facts: for no thoughtful historian, no matter how personally skeptical he may be of the Faith, can fairly deny that the life and death of Christ has divided human history as nothing else has done.

Before that central point, humanity seemed to be sinking ever deeper and deeper into misery and sin; any increase in civilisation apparently meaning only increased facilities for viciousness, and the infliction of wrong. Men felt the gross darkness of their sins growing deeper and denser around them, while their religions and philosophies had lost their power to aid; their only hope being in that eagerly expected Advent of the God-man, Who should renew the "Golden Age."

Then at the darkest hour the dawn came—the "Sun of Righteousness arose with healing in His wings;"—and the path of humanity was no longer downwards, but upwards to God through Him. True, "man's inhumanity to man" is, unhappily, rife enough, even now; and sin and suffering have by no means ceased upon this earth; nevertheless it is a fact that the tide of righteousness is rising; and that men, by reason of Christ and His Church, are ever becoming better, and purer, and happier; so that we can fairly anticipate the day when "the Kingdoms of this world" shall have become "the Kingdoms of our Lord, and of His Christ."

There is yet another aspect, that ought not to be overlooked, in which we may recognise our Lord as the pivotal center of history; and that is in the political and social, no less than the religious, preparation of heathendom for His Advent, and His Church.

Thus we may instance the unifying policy of Rome, fusing away the barriers between men; and thus completing the work begun by the preceding empires of Babylon, Persia, and Macedon: for from this unification sprang, as we know, that destructive syncretism of the National Religions that, humanly speaking, rendered possible the triumphs of Christianity; and so too, again, was evolved that conception of "world-citizenship," that both enabled the Gospel to be preached; and also made comprehensible its doctrines of the brotherhood of men, the Fatherhood of God and the unity of humanity in our Lord and Saviour Christ.

And so, again, even now, may we still recognise in human affairs, if we will but look for it, this constant preparation for, and furtherance of, the work of Christ, and His Church.

True, this is a line of argument that must, evidently, vary greatly in cogency, according as it is moulded, both by our acquaintance with the philosophy of history, and also by the individual bias of our mind. Nevertheless it is surely not too much to say that there has been, and is, this preparation of heathendom for Christianity—of heathendom as it existed before Christ came, of heathendom as it exists now in non-Christian lands, aye! and of heathendom as it exists still, by reason of human iniquity, in the midst of our highest civilization.

And here let me remark that no thoughtful theologian can fail to see, in this preparation of the nations for the Christ, the definite operation of that Indwelling and Inspiring Holy Spirit, Who Eternally Proceedeth through the Son; working upon the nations by the gift of the Logos, as He works upon the Church by the gift of the Christ (vide p. 71); brooding o'er their discords with His life giving wings, as He brooded over chaos at the building of the world.

But since there is this preparation of humanity for Christ—since He is this central pivot of the Ages, no less than the Great Logos of the "λόγοι," and Revealer of God to man,—since, in short, He is this King over the souls of men, we may well ask how He could be merely "David's son."

Surely the mighty facts of His life, and of His work, are only intelligible under the Catholic doctrine of His Person, namely that He—the "Son of man"—was the Incarnate Primal Adam, and Archetypal Logos of God; Who for us men, and for our salvation, came down from heaven, took our true nature upon Him, and was born as Man among men.

NOTE FOURTEEN

ON THE "LOCAL MANIFESTATION" OF OUR LORD.

THE doctrine that I have enunciated in my treatise, concerning the Incarnation and "Kenosis" of our Lord—namely that the said Incarnation and "Kenosis" was, in no sense, a "laying aside" of His Divinity; but merely a necessarily visible, temporal, and local "manifestation" and limitation by that Incarnation of Him Who was both previously, and simultaneously the Invisible Eternal, Omnipresent, and Omnipotent Logos—this doctrine, I say, is not only taught by our Lord (vide St. John, iii, 13), but is also something that must, perforce, be evident to any one who, in any degree, appreciates the Catholic doctrines of the Triune Nature, and Immanence in His creation of God, and as such a necessary deduction, it was unhesitatingly accepted by all the old Fathers of the Church.

Thus, to give a few brief extracts from some of the principal authorities, we may instance the following.

St. Athanasius (De Incar: Verbi Dei; § 17). "For He was not, as might be imagined, circumscribed in the body; nor while present in the body, was He absent elsewhere; nor while He moved the body, was the Universe left void of His working and providence;" * * * "for just as, while present in the whole of Creation, He is at once distinct in being from the Universe, and present in all things by His power" * * * "thus, even while present in a human body, and Himself quickening it, He was, without inconsistency, quickening the Universe as well, and was in every process of nature, and yet also outside of the whole; and while known from the body by His works, He was not the less manifest from the working of the Universe as a whole." * * * "And this was the wonderful thing, that He was at once walking as man, and, as the Word, was quickening all things, and, as the Son, was dwelling with His Father."

St. Hilary (De Trinit: iii, 16). "Non amiserat quod erat sed coeperat esse quod non erat; non de suo destiterat, sed quod nostrum est acceperat;" (ix, 66.) "Nec Deus destitit manere qui homo est;" (xi, 48) "In forma enim Dei manens, forma servi assumpsit" * * * (xii, 6) "neque enim defecit ex sese qui se evacuavit."

St. Epiphanius (Adv. Haer: Lib. ii, Haer. lxix, cap. 61). καὶ ἐν Μαρίᾳ ἐτύγχανε καὶ ἄνθρωπος ἐγένετο, ἀλλὰ τῇ δυνάμει ἀυτοῦ ἐπλήρου τὰ σύμπαντα.

St. Augustine (Epist: 137 ad Volusianum. c. ii, 6). "Et putamus nobis de omnipotentia Dei incredibile dici aliquid, cum dicitur Verbum Dei, per quod omnia facta sunt, sic assumpsisse corpus ex Virgine, et sensibus apparuisse mortalibus, ut immortalitatem suam non corruperit, ut aeternitatem non mutaverit, ut potestatem non minuerit, ut administrationem mundi non deseruerit, ut a sinu Patris, id est a secreto, quo cum illo, et in illo est, non recesserit" * * * (Cap iii, 10). "Homo quippe Deo accessit, non Deus a Se recessit;" and in Epist. CXL. cap. 3.

"Hic ergo Deus, Verbum Dei per quod facta sunt omnia, Filius Dei est, incommutabiliter manens, ubique praesens, nullo clausus loco, nec partialiter per cuncta diffusus"; and in "De Fide, ad Petr:" cap. 2, similarly. Vide also Tract: in Joan, ii, 4; xvii, 16; cii, 6; cxi, 2, etc.; and in Epist: cxl, cap. 3.

St. Gregory Nazianzen (Epist. CI. "to Cledonius the priest, against Apollinarius") "Who (i. e. the Eternal Word) in these last days has assumed manhood also for our salvation; passible in His flesh, impassible in His Godhead; circumscript in the body, uncircumscript in the Spirit, etc., etc."

St. Gregory of Nyssa, who (in his "Cat: Magna. Cap. X.) denies that the Infinity of the Godhead could be circumscribed by the Incarnation; for that would be an impossibility.

Theodoret ("On the Immutability of the Word." cap. I.) shows that, inasmuch as the Word is "per se" immutable, He therefore must be said to have *assumed* flesh in the Incarnation; not *become* flesh, as the Monophysites taught: and again in the "Dialogue on the Unconfounded," cap. II., he argues similarly: and yet again, in his Eccl. History (Book V, c. xi) he quotes, as orthodox, "a Confession of the Catholic Faith, which Pope Damascus sent to Bishop Paulinus in Macedonia, when he was at Thessalonica" in which the following passage occurs, "If any one says that the Son of God, living in the flesh when He was on earth, was not in heaven, and with the Father, let him be anathema."

St. John Damascene (De Fide. Orth: lib. iii, cap. ii.). "' ἀλλ' ἐνόικήσας τῇ γαστρὶ τῆς ἁγίας Παρθένου, ἀπεριγράπτως ἐν τῇ ἑαυτοῦ ὑποστάσει" * * * [Cap. vii] " ἐπ' ἐσχάτων δὲ τῶν Πατρικῶν κόλπων οὐκ 'ἀποστάντα Λόγον, 'ἀπεριγράπτως, ἐνῳκηκένοι τῇ γαστρὶ τῆς ἁγίας Παρθένου, 'ἀσπόρως κ. τ. λ."

St. Thomas Aquinas (Sum. Theo. Pars. iii, Q. v, art. 2, ad. 1). "Christus dicitur de coelo descendisse dupliciter. Uno modo ratione Divinae Naturae: non ita quod Natura Divina in coelo desierit, sed quia in infimis novo modo esse coepit; scilicet secundum naturam assumptam, secundum illud Joan iii, 13;" etc. Vide also notes 38, 104, 110, on the "descent into Hell," and note 119 on the "Ascension."

See also St. Irenaeus (Con:Haer. v, 18, 3); Origen ("De Princip." trans. by Rufinus, Book iv, 30; and "Com. in Joan," Tom. vi,; ed. of Migne, 1862, pp. 264, 265); Eusebius ("Dem. Evang.," lib. iv, 13, and vii, 1); Proclus of Cyzicus ("Orat. I, 9," ed. of

Migne. LXV, p. 690); John Cassian ("De Incar:" vi, 19; and "The Seven books of John Cassian," iv, 6; vii, 22. etc., etc. "The Conf. of Abbot Moses," c. xiv); St. Leo. (Epist. xxviii, "to Flavian," i. e. "the Tome"); St. Ambrose (De Spiritu Sancto, Book I, cap. 9), etc., etc.

In short this truth of the "local manifestation" was never lost sight of, or denied, either by the Fathers, or the Schoolmen; although, doubtless, in many cases its prime importance, for an accurate conception of the Incarnation, does not seem to be quite so clearly apprehended as it was, say, by St. Athanasius.

Nevertheless, whether enlarged upon, or not, it was always distinctly recognised as an integral part of Catholic doctrine; and the opposite dangers of Monophysitism, on the one hand, and either Nestorianism, or Doketism, on the other — or in other words, the blending of the human and the Divine, or the failure of a true Incarnation—that Scylla and Charybdis of Christology, were thereby avoided.

But at the period of the "Reformation," Lutheranism, by its Monophysitic formula of "nec Verbum extra carnem, nec caro extra Verbum," distinctly contradicted this necessary doctrine; and thus became the logical parent of such absurd and painful theories of the Incarnation, and its "Kenosis," as those advocated by Zinzendorf, Gess, and others (vide pp. 12 and 21 and note 12); for their thoroughly "Trideistic" theory is, as I have said (note 12), only explicable as the joint product of Lutheran Monophysitism, and eighteenth century Deism.[127]

Calvin, on the other hand, in opposition to Lutheranism, reproduced, on this point, the teachings of St. Thomas Aquinas (vide his Inst., Book ii, c. xv); and, as a consequence, Presbyterian and Calvinistic theology has always retained a more or less clear expression of it; although Calvin's horrible doctrine that Christ, during His Crucifixion, was "under the wrath of God!" has practically nullified this acknowledgment by again introducing a "Trideistic" separation of wills between the Personalities of the Blessed Trinity.

Returning to the succession of Catholic theologians—i. e., in the Roman Communion, and in our own Anglican branch,—[128] I may say that even here, to the best of my knowledge, this vital element in the theology of the Incarnation, has not been given in any sense, formally rejected, or denied; but simply that it has the place and attention it deserves; but has been, practically, at any rate, overlooked; I do not mean, of course, that it has been, been, as I have just stated, overlooked; almost the only recogni-

---

(127) Yet, on the other hand, Martensen, the Danish Lutheran Bishop, in his "Christliche Dogmatik" [pp. 266–7], gives the clearest and most accurate expression to the doctrine of the "Local Manifestation" that, to my knowledge, has appeared of late years.

(128) Concerning modern Greek and Russian theology, I regret to say that I am far too ignorant of the subject to speak of its bearing upon this point.

tion it receives being in connection with the "descent into Hell," when such notice can not well be avoided.

But although it has been so, practically, neglected, yet it is, manifestly, a doctrine of the utmost importance; for until we clearly recognise it in all its bearings, and give it the prominence that is its due, much in the theology of the Incarnation will seem self contradictory, and untenable: but once let it be thoroughly grasped and realised, and not only will our theological concepts gain in clearness and accuracy, but also, as a necessary consequence, will our vital grasp upon, and personal relation to, the great verities of our Faith be strengthened and made sure.

On the other hand, I utterly fail to see how any "communicatio idiomatum" can properly be predicated in the Incarnation.

True it is that many elements in our Lord's character—such as His holiness, His love, and even His obedience to the will of the Father—are equally predicable of both His Natures—His Logos Godhead, and His real humanity.—And even furthermore; as I have shown (vide Chap. V.), the said holiness, love, and obedience, as also our Lord's human wisdom, partook of such a perfect and inerrant character, as they never could have hoped to have attained, were their "hypostatic Ego" not the Divine Logos of God: so that, in some small sense, it may be truly said that our Lord's humanity participated, to some extent, in one, at least, of the prerogatives of His Divinity, namely Inerrancy.

Yet notwithstanding, all this holiness, love, obedience, and knowledge were not, in any sense, "idiomata" unnatural and foreign to the humanity; but were, on the contrary, qualities entirely natural to the man; being, in short, essential parts of that "image" of the Logos, in which man had first been made; and therefore wholly proper to humanity.

In fact, as I have shown in my main treatise (Chap. IV), it was entirely on account of this likeness—this common ground—between man and his God, that the Logos was able to be Incarnate, and live as very man (vide p. 47). This being so, there was, then, in these "common properties," manifestly, no true "communicatio idiomatum," in any sense of the term; but merely the necessary fact that those things which became Him in His Godhead, also became Him as very and true man.

But, it may be asked, was not the Inerrancy which, as noted above, was conveyed by His Divinity to those natural human qualities of holiness and knowledge, as they existed in Christ, was not this a real "communicatio" from the Divine Estate?

To this we may reply by pointing out that the said Inerrancy was merely perfect in degree; inasmuch as it was circumscribed by the real and finite humanity—or in other words, that it was not such an Absolute Omniscience and Holiness, as is only proper to the non-Incarnate Divinity: but merely such a relative perfection as is, not only predicable, but essentially proper both to the Ideal man, and to God in Man.—Even the Inerrancy, then, conveyed to His human powers by our Lord, can not be properly described as a "communicatio idiomatum;" but rather as a mere "communication of *power*," developing the "idiomata" that were native to man.

In brief, then, as I have stated on page 47 of my main treatise, whatever our Lord did in His Incarnation, that He evidently did as the Incarnate One, and therefore *solely as man;* it follows from this that all the above perfections, although certainly suitable to His Godhead, were yet not wrought by Him as God, but as man; for in His character and life there was no alternation of parts; nor even a simultaneous co-working; but a constant acting as the Incarnate.

But if there was no true blending in the common properties of our Lord's Two Natures, still less was there any communication of the "idiomata" peculiar to each. For His manhood certainly did not, and could not, receive any of the powers peculiar to the Godhead—such as Omniscience, Omnipresence, or Omnipotence; —any statement contradicting this elementary fact would, surely, involve us in all the philosophical absurdities of the Monophysite heresy.

But if His manhood did not receive any of the properties of His Godhead, still less is it possible to conceive of that Godhead as partaking in any of the "idiomata" peculiar to the manhood—such as its finiteness, its passibility, and its liability to temptation,—and thus ceasing to be the Absolute. This absurdity, I trust, I have fully refuted in treating of the Neo-Monophysitic heresies of Zinzendorf, Gess, and Ebrard (vide p. 21).

And finally, even if we explain the "communicatio" in the usual Catholic sense, as merely meaning that "whatever belongs to our Lord in either of His Two Natures, belongs to Him as the One Christ," even in this case, I say, the phrase must not be logically pressed; as otherwise it might imply that there was constituted of those "Two Natures" a Monophysitic "third something," to which the said Natures communicated their "idiomata."

In short, the theory that there is any "communicatio idiomatum" whatever between our Lord's Two Natures is, to my mind, a theory that darkens, rather than illumines; for if there be any meaning at all in the words, it can only imply such a Monophysitic confusion between the Godhead and the manhood as is clearly absurd and heretical.

In making these strong assertions I am, of course, aware that many of the Fathers and Schoolmen have employed the phrase; but I believe I am correct in stating that, in spite of its occasional use, it is yet a formula that is extraneous to their general tone of thought;[190] and one that they never sounded, or developed:

---

(190) Thus, to take but three representative men St. Cyril of Alex: (Scholia De Incar: cap. 11), St. John Damascene (De Fide Orth: Lib: iii, cap. 4), and St. Thomas

I do not think that any of them ever attached any importance to the phrase; or would hesitate for a moment, to reject it if the issue were clearly drawn.

In fact it was ever, if I may be allowed the expression, a mere conventional and perfunctory phrase, that was only employed to evade (shall I say) difficulties in the exposition of our Lord's character—such as His cry upon the Cross;—whose true solution lies, not in any such fancied "communicatio," but rather, as I have endeavored to show in my treatise, in the full appreciation and application of the "local manifestation and limitation" of our Lord, caused by His real Incarnation.

Aquinas (Sum: Theo: Pars iii. Q. xvi, art. 5), all vehemently deny that there was any interchange, or confusion whatever between the Divine, and the human "idiomata" of our Lord.

NOTE THIRTY-ONE

ON THE HYPOSTATIC UNION IN CHRIST.

IT is highly important to notice that the word "hypostasis" is used in Christian theology in two widely different and almost opposite senses, according as it relates to the doctrine of the Trinity, or has reference to the union of Two Natures in our Lord.

In its etymology, and primitive use, as every Greek scholar knows, "$\dot{υ}πόστασις$" exactly corresponded to the Latin "substantia" or substratum, and was equivalent, in all respects, to the "$ο\dot{υ}σ\tilde{ι}α$" or "real being" of a thing as it is "in itself."

But in the formulation of the Church's doctrine of the Trinity, both it, and "$πρόσωπον$" were at first used to express the Three Personalities of the One God; the quasi-Monarchian faultiness of the one expression (i. e. "$πρόσωπον$") being used to balance and correct the quasi-Tritheistic faultiness of the other (i. e. "$\dot{υ}πόστασις$"). But evidently this state of acknowledged faulty expression could not continue; the Church, both for its own sake, and for that of the heretics, must have an exact terminology; and hence, shortly after the Council of Nicaea, the use of "$πρόσωπον$" was entirely abandoned, and "$\dot{υ}πόστασις$" given the specialised and technical meaning of a "Personality" in the Blessed Trinity; its former meaning of "substantia" or substratum being abrogated in this connection.

But when the various Christological heresies shortly after arose, "$\dot{υ}πόστασις$" was again used for the relation that existed between the Incarnate Logos, and His humanity; and, in this case, retained its old pre-Nicene meaning of "substantia;" for, as it was explained, just as the creative and hypostatic Spirit, or "Ego," together with its begotten "mind," and created and material "body," made one man; so the Creative and Hypostatic Logos of God, together with the begotten "mind," and created material "body," of the real humanity of our Lord, made One Christ; Who thus "hypostatically" joined His humanity to His Divinity.

This wide difference, then, of meaning between the Trinitarian "$\dot{υ}πόστασις$," and the Christological "$\dot{υ}πόστασις$," must, in no case, be overlooked, or forgotten; inasmuch as upon its clear appreciation depends our accurate grasp of Catholic truth.

THREE ESSAYS

SUBSIDIARY

TO THE

DOCTRINE OF THE INCARNATION

ON THE

ESSENTIAL NATURE OF SIN

SPIRIT AND MATTER

AND

THE PRIMARY CRITERION OF TRUTH

On the Essential Nature of Sin

THE realization of sin—of our wrong doing and unworthiness before God—is one of the most persistent experiences in our moral and spiritual natures: we naturally wish to be happy, to be free from care, and self satisfied; and yet, in spite of these powerful interests to the contrary, we are incessantly distressed by this sense of culpability—by this testimony of our consciences that we have repeatedly broken the laws of our deepest nature, and of our God.—The question, then, as to why we are sinners, and what, in its essential nature is "sin," this question, I say, has ever possessed an absorbing and vital interest to earnest and thoughtful men.

The earliest attempt to solve this problem consisted in the theory that "sin," in its essence, was simply *sensuousness* or in other words, the deference of a man to the merely animal guidance of his appetites.

This theory, while fundamentally false, as I will show, in its ultimate analysis, yet contains enough superficial verity to be readily accepted by primitive thought: for the most obvious sins—those whose evil effects were most evident,—were precisely those that partook of this sensual character; gluttony, drunkenness, debauchery, all such sinkings as these of the man in his animal nature, were so evidently wrong, both in themselves, and in their effects, that it was easy to think of these alone as sins, and to overlook the far more heinous, and entirely nonsensual evils of dishonesty, envy, and malice.

Tracing onward this idea of sin as "sensuousness"—the swaying of a man by his animal instincts and passions,—we may say that its logical outcome was Gnostic and Manichaean Dualism, and ultimately also the Nihilism of the Buddhist.

Thus, taking up Gnosticism in the first place, we may say that evil having been identified with animality, it was natural that man should be divided into two sharply antithetical and opposite natures—one sensual, "material," sinful, and dead; and the other anti-sensual, "spiritual," holy and living.

Following on this division, it was equally natural that the same antithesis should be carried out into Nature; until the only conceivable relation that the Pure Supreme Spirit could be thought to have with dead and polluted "matter" was by means of successive "Emanations,"[130] with their successive deteriorations; until at least a "Demiurge" was evolved, gross enough to meddle with "matter," and create the world. And logically, furthermore, this "Demiurge," as the maker of the material Universe, was the Author also of sin; and we thus arrive at the complete Dualistic theory of Two opposed Creators — the "Demiurge," and the "Primal Spirit,"—with their two equally opposed, and mutually exclusive Universes, the one entirely evil, and the other entirely good.

The error of all this is obvious; for, as the Early Fathers of the Church, in their fight against Gnosticism, showed, it lay open to the vital objection of opposing, as mutually incompatible, God and His world: it introduced, in short, a spirit of falsity into Nature; making it the work of a lying demon, in place of the Universe of God.

It furthermore, by its theory of two contrasted Universes, rendered any redemption of the sinner an utter impossibility; for, evidently, what was evil must remain such; and what was good could not be altered; any passage, then, or transition between the two opposite worlds was plainly unthinkable.

And lastly, it made the gross philosophical error of treating "sin" as if it were a concrete, and separate entity; in place of its being, as it is, a mere question of *relation*, and of the *will*.

So much, then, for the Gnostic theory of evil as inherent in matter, qua matter; a theory that is, as I have shown, derived from the primal mistake of identifying "sin" with "sensuousness."

But from this conception, again, was also evolved, as I have stated, the Buddhistic doctrine of Nihilism. For evil being thought to have its origin in the material body and its senses, all that gave life and being to that bodily existence was considered, by a simple train of reasoning, to be also evil, in that it was the sustainer and originator of sin. Therefore love, hate, thought, desire, will—all things, in short, that gave individuality to the man, and differentiated him, in any way, from the universe around him—were all considered to be sinful "per se;" in that they were, simply and solely, instances of an existence, "material" in character, and separate from "Pure Spirit;" and, therefore, wholly sinful in its being.

The wisest and holiest thing, then, under this supposition, that a man could do was to so weaken and impoverish that sinful individuality, by the suppression of all natural emotion and desire— erring as little on the side of undue mortification, as of self indulgence; but holding the middle course of placid passivity,— that when this prison house of flesh, now binding him to "delusion"—to "Maya,"—dropped away in death, his spirit might

---

(130) Which, I need hardly remark, implied, not merely *Procession*, and certainly not *Plenary Derivation* (like the Catholic doctrine of the "Begetting," and "Procession" of the Son, and Holy Spirit), but rather, as I state in the text, Procession with *deterioration*.

retain nothing of its stain; but free from desire, thought, or will, be assimilated into the Pure Being of the Universe, "as a bursting bubble is absorbed in the ocean where it floats;" and thus would be attained the final rest of "Nirvana."[131]

But if, on the other hand, a person did not so quench the delusive fires of life—the desires and emotions of his senses,—but, on the contrary, gave them full sway over his being, by loving, by hating, by thinking, by willing, and above all, by indulging the desires of the flesh, then he would so ingrain into his nature that individuality — that sinful separateness from "Undifferentiated Being"—as to render impossible his absorption after death into the restful bosom of the Universe. Necessity — "Karma" — would then condemn him to a new era of life—a metempsychosis —a re-incarnation;—possibly, if his animality was strong, even in the being of a beast. So the weary round would go on, birth upon birth, life after life, until at last he would awaken to the truth, quench his desires, destroy his individuality, and so, at death, reach the final haven of "Nirvana."

Now all this is evidently self nugatory, illogical, and untenable; inasmuch as in denouncing individuality, it denounces also the very foundations of its own reasoning. For if all thought, and all existence be but an lying dream, must not Buddhistic thought itself be equally a lie? And if, again, we predicate the "Unconscious" as the Ultimate Reality of Being, must we not either rank "tree life" (so to speak) above the intelligent life of a man; or else conceive of thought and will as the creations and products of that "Blind Life!" And finally, is it not the height of absurdity to treat life, and all that makes life possible—namely thought, love, will, and personality,—as if it were the negation of being; and call abstract negation "the only true life!"

Buddhistic Pessimism and Nihilism is, then, I repeat, self nugatory, illogical, and utterly untenable; and yet it is, as I have just shown, simply the logical outcome of the initial mistake of conceiving of "sin" solely as "sensuousness;" with its necessary Dualistic deductions of a "per se" evilness of "matter," and two opposite worlds.

But even further: this same erroneous conception of "sin" as "material," and "material" as "sin," with its logical Manichaean corolleries of an "evil world of nature" opposed to a "good world

---

[131] Which, as I may remark, is *not*, as it is so often mistakenly explained, *annihilation*; but is rather absorption into "το πᾶν." Buddhism, in fact, with its doctrine of the Ultimate Pure Undifferentiated Being, from Which was evolved all the fantastic worlds of gods and of men, and to Which, at last, they finally return and are re-absorbed, in this conception, I say, it closely approximated to the "Ultimate Unconscious" of Schopenhaur and Hartmann—that Great "Tree Life" (so to speak) of the Universe, which is, as these philosophers imagine, the Ultimate Reality, and Cause of All.

Furthermore; their common deduction, from these premises, of pessimistic and hopeless conclusions is especially striking; and the same objections of self contradiction, and suicidal negation, are valid against both systems.

In fact the pessimistic "Philosophy of the Unconscious" is, in all vital respects, only Buddhism in a new guise; as, indeed, its advocates have frankly allowed.

of spirit," reappears in a very prevalent modern theory of ethics, and "spiritual religion;" a theory that can, perhaps, be most conveniently named the "Puritanical" one.

This, in its prime origin, sprang from the extreme fatalism of the various "reformers"—Luther, Melancthon, Calvin, Zwingli, Beza, etc.,—and their consequent conception of sin as essential to the nature of man, *as man;* so that *all* his acts—his prayers, and his virtues, no whit less than his vices—were wholly and entirely sin, and created as such by God; an evilness that was so essential to our being that it remained untouched and unaltered, even after a man was forensically "counted righteous" by God![132]

This general system reverses it will be noticed, the Gnostic and Buddhistic progression; for while these latter reasoned from the supposed sensuous character of sin, to pessimism and fatalism, Lutheranism and Puritanism argued from fatalism, to a practically dualistic theory of sin and the world.

According to this system, then, "grace" or "spirituality," instead of being a coherent prolongation of, and in agreement with nature (vide pp. 42, 43, and note 71), was completely and entirely opposed to it in all respects; whatsoever things were "natural," being therefore "per se" evil; and whatsoever things were "spiritual," being therefore "per se" anti-natural. In agreement with this view the Biblical doctrine of the "fall of man" was taken out of its proper subsidiary position, and made the central and all important fact of religion, hiding or distorting everything else; man, under this teaching, being no longer in the "image" of his God—a "lost piece of *silver*"—a "wandering *sheep*"—a "prodigal *son*";—but rather an "utter mass of corruption"—a reprobate and devil,—totally delivered to evil, and belonging (in the language of the Gnostics) to a world that was "ὑλική"—sensual and vile! Whatsoever things, then, as I have already stated, that were "natural" to the man—his "virtues," no less than his "vices"—were thought to be in themselves essentially and irredeemably evil; and especially was this true of his pleasures and enjoyments; for inasmuch as these were so agreeable and helpful to corrupt humanity they must, manifestly, be totally wrong and vile.

The only course, then, proper to a spiritual man—i. e. one who had been arbitrarily and unwillingly transferred by God (or perhaps, more strictly, treated as if transferred)[133] from the evil world of "nature," to the opposite world of "spirit"—the only course, I say, for such a one to adopt, with regard to this sinful world and its pleasures, was, either to avoid them, as far as possible, and so

---

(132) That I have not overdrawn, or overstated in *any* way this horrible common feature of the systems of the various "Reformers," will, I think, be allowed by any one who has even the most cursory acquaintance with their writings. For some examples, see Luther [Com: in Gal: cap. ii, 20, and v, 19], Melancthon [Com: in Romans], Calvin [Inst: Lib: ii, cap. 2, §§ 1, 9, &c.], Beza [Aphorisms], Zwingli [De Provid: cap. 6], &c., &c.

(133) Inasmuch as his evil nature was thought to be entirely unaffected; all his acts, even his very prayers, being still essentially and wholly *sin*.

be "unnatural;" or else, seeing that this abnegation of nature, manifestly, cannot be perfectly accomplished (especially as the transfer to the "spiritual" kingdom was only fictitious, not actual), to freely indulge in them all without let or hindrance, recognising the fact that it was only the hopelessly carnal and evil nature that could be affected thereby; the "spirituality" remaining entirely unaffected, and possessed of indefeasible grace.

In accordance with this truly horrible scheme, God was no longer thought of as the Immanent Father of Nature, loving all, and Eternally working in His Cosmos; but rather as an external Power, separate from all; only at times arbitrarily interfering with Nature; and then only to work in opposition and contradiction to its laws."[134] And furthermore; inasmuch as God was so entirely alien from Nature and its "logoi," He ought then to be worshipped, by His favourites, in as ugly, as barren, and as unnatural a manner as possible—the "beauty of holiness" having no longer any meaning;—all music, all colors, all flowers, all ritual, being manifestly "natural" and "material;" and therefore essentially "unspiritual," "ungodly," and wrong!

This damnable heresy, as a whole, is, thank Heaven, largely dying away; but yet we may still observe traces of its influence in the objection so frequently urged, even now, against the ritual and Sacraments of the Church, namely that they are "material;" and therefore necessarily "unspiritual," and opposed to all true worship.

And so too have we still to suffer from the "tender consciences," and far from tender tongues, of ill-educated people; who think our innocent pleasures — our golf, our athletics, or our games — "worldly," and "unworthy of serious professors" (to use their own uncouth phraseology), far exceeding in heinousness any malicious scandal in which they may choose to indulge; and we, for refusing such a standard, are thereby incontrovertibly convicted of "ungodliness;" or else are thought to be, at the very least, "shallow in our personal religion."

And so, yet again, are many of the erroneous popular conceptions of Christianity directly traceable to this Puritanical Dualism. Thus we constantly meet the false spirituality that abuses the body as a clog—a hindrance—of the soul, and that speaks of death as a "going to glory;" thus ignoring, and sometimes even openly denying, the Catholic doctrines, both of the estate of the soul in Hades (vide pp. 62-64), and of the resurrection of our bodies from the dead.

In fact it is not too much to say that the ultimate root of most, if not all, modern heresies, from "revivalism," on the one hand,

---

(134) Canon Gore, in his "Bampton Lectures" on the Incarnation [p. 110], speaks of 'the tendency, always present in the vulgar imagination, to see the Divine, rather in what is portentous and unaccountable, than in what is orderly and tranquil. To think of power, not as what works through law, but as what triumphs over it."

to the so-called "liberalism," on the other, is this essential Dualism inherited from Puritanism. Thus, to illustrate, we have on the one side the "revival" conception of religion as belonging solely to men of a certain artificial nature—namely the "godly" or "spiritual"—who have "experienced religion;"—the race of man, as a whole, being thought to be merely "natural" and "worldly;" and to have therefore no concern whatever in the matter, or relationship with the Great Father of All! Surely this, as I may remark in passing, is an accursed heresy: God is the Father of *all* and His redemption is for *every* man; for none are "ὑλικοὶ" and vile. True it is that men are practically divided into two classes—"Christian," and "non-Christian,"—just as they are into "Republican," and "non-Republican," or "English" and "non-English;" but the difference lies solely in their circumstances, and wills; and is, in no sense, a matter of essential nature; for all are in the "image" of God; and all therefore, and *only therefore*, can be redeemed by Him.

But turning from "revivalism" to the modern "liberalism," we find the same fundamental confusion of "spirituality" with "unnaturalness;" only in this instance "unnaturalness" means unreality and self delusion. Thus prayer is made a mere emotional exercise; and religion "undogmatic," and wholly subjective; until we finally issue in a Christianity that is a mere "impressional atmosphere;" and a God and Christ Who "only exists in the hearts of the faithful;" and is, in short, such a mere auto-projection of humanity as is the "Etre Supreme" of "Positivism."

And all these protean forms of error are, I repeat, the mere logical expression and outcome of Puritanical habits of thought, with their "quasi Gnostic" theories of the evilness of the world, and the material character of sin.

But, as I need scarcely point out, it is all radically and fundamentally wrong. Religion and Spirituality are not synonymous with delusion and unreality; man and Nature are not the creations and offspring of the Evil One; and natural emotions and pleasures are not "per se" sinful and wrong; but are, on the contrary "per se" entirely right, just so far as they may be in agreement with the Cosmos of the Universe, and our own true nature.[135] "Spirit" and "matter," in short, are not two contradictory and mutually exclusive worlds; but are, on the contrary, two perfectly congruous, and mutually dependent "Cosmoi;" being created, and ruled by the same Lord and Father of all; this thought I will more fully develop in the succeeding Essay upon "Spirit and Matter."

The theory, then, of "sin" being simply "sensuousness," or in other words, inherent in the body and its senses, is an utterly un-

---

(135) But see pp. 60, and 66, and note 114, and my remarks there on the discords that have been introduced into our nature by sin. All our desires, then, may not be equally "Cosmical," or, in other words, equally in agreement with our *true* nature: but may, on the contrary, be the unnatural products of either "habitual," or "original" sin—or, in other words, of acquired, or inherited evil tastes.

tenable one; for it leads us, as we have seen, into the illogical and destructive quagmires of Dualism, of Nihilism, or of Puritanical misconceptions of the Faith. It is, in short, while superficially attractive, yet based upon an essentially shallow, and entirely false view.

For although a sensuous act may be, and often is, exceedingly sinful and wrong, sinking the man even lower than the animal existences around him; yet the sin of the act consists, as I will show, simply and solely, in its spiritual relations; for in so far as it is merely "sensual"—or a following of the senses—it is, manifestly, in complete accord with our nature; and therefore, as I have stated above, entirely right and true.

On the other hand, as I have already hinted at the beginning of this Essay, those sins that are most heinous and "mortal" in their nature—that destroy most quickly the "image" of the Logos in the soul (vide p. 60)—are precisely those that partake of an entirely "spiritual" character. Envy, hatred, and malice, cruelty, hypocrisy, dishonesty, and lies, all these are, assuredly, "non-sensual" in their nature, and belong wholly to the spirit; and furthermore, as I would like to point out, the more "spiritual" they are—the more they rise superior to the bodily senses, and the individual—in fact (if we may use the term), the more "*unselfish*" they are,—the more horrible, fiendish, and devilish they also become.

"Sin" then is, in its essential character, in no sense a material thing dependent, for its being, on the body and the bodily senses; but is, on the contrary, an entirely spiritual relation, dependent solely on the will.

Referring back to what I have said in my main treatise (pp. 40 et seq.) upon the necessity of temptation to man, it will there be seen that "sin," as a result of temptation, must be a necessary possibility (but only *possibility*, not *certainty*) to him. For inasmuch as man is both a self centered, and a finite individual—is, in other words, both endowed with a "free will" or "self determination," and is also necessarily ignorant and limited at many points—he can, and must, continually exercise his essential power of choice; and therefore, as I have said, must be continually exposed to temptation, and liable to fall into sin; until he has, by experience, attained the protection of a "habit of righteousness." Apollinarius, therefore, in holding that sin belonged by nature to every finite will (vide p. 18), only made the mistake (but that a most vital one) of turning a "necessary *may be*" into a "necessary *must*."

This being so, then "sin," in its initial stage, can, perhaps, be best described as an imperfection—a falling short of truth and righteousness—a choosing of the wrong path, or even of the "lesser good."

And furthermore; it is the amount of this imperfection—this

falling short—this defect of good,—and it alone, that determines the sinfulness of the sin. From this it follows that "sins of omission," and of "commission," are only catechetically separable; inasmuch as every sin, at its ultimate analysis, is, as I have said, an omission, or negation of good.

This being so, we can, then, well understand how so many able theologians, from St. Augustine,[136] and the "Areopagite,"[137] to the "schoolmen" of the Middle Ages,[138] have called "sin" a mere negation—a "στέρησις;"—and likened it to darkness—the absence and negation of light.—And this, too, is, I think, the point of Isaiah's statement (chap. xlv, 7), where he takes the chosen similitude of the Magians between evil and darkness, and shows it to be entirely misapplied; inasmuch as neither darkness, nor evil were such concrete entities as they imagined; but were rather negative relations, solely dependent for their existence on the being of their opposite realities—light, and good;—for "I," the Lord, "form the light, and create darkness; I make peace, and create evil."

In fact, we may say that this must needs be true; for it is a familiar axiom in logic that the opposite of a thing can be no real entity, but only a negation. Thus the opposite of "white" is "not white," or as we generally describe it, "black:" and so too the opposite of "red" is, it is true, "green;" but this is not as the *color* "green," but as a "not red." Similarly, then, the opposite of "good" can only be "not good;" and if "evil" is also an opposite, it must therefore be simply an interchangeable term.

"Sin," therefore, is initially a "not good"—a "falling short;"—but yet it cannot consist merely in this "falling short"—this "failure to attain;"—for if it did, it would hardly be culpable, or worthy of the reprobation of God. The Father can, certainly, condemn none of His finite creatures for a mere want of knowledge, or ability—of Omniscience, or Omnipotence;—inasmuch as, by their very essential being, they cannot but be ignorant, and powerless at many points. But while He cannot, then, condemn us for mere passive ignorance, and passive failure to attain, yet He certainly can for an active and deliberate falling short, and a refusal of offered guidance and light; and this is, in fact, the key of the whole question.

In the heart of every man, as man,[139] is shining the "Logos light"—in all cases, the "light of reason," and of "conscience;" and in some worthy cases, the further "light of grace;"—and from Him, too, comes that wonderful faculty of love, by which we are drawn into sympathy and union with our fellows, and with our God.

---

(116) Vide the "Enchiridion." cap. 11-14.
(137) "On the Divine Names." Book iv. § 34.
(138) E. g. St. Thomas Aquinas [Sum: Theo: Pars ia. Q. xliv, art. 1 and 2; and ia, IIae, Q. clx, art. 2. ad. 2], &c. Vide also St. Gregory of Nyssa ["De Anima et Resur:" and "De Cat: Magna," cap 6]. St. Athanasius [contra Gentes, §§ 2-7]. &c.
(139) Vide note 1, and pp. 2, 3, 42 and 43. &c., of the main treatise, "De Incarnatione."

When, therefore, the choice comes to a man, by which he must decide the path that he will tread, he has, for his right guidance, this indefectible, unalterable, and (to his finite capacity) absolutely true "light of reason," of "conscience," and of "grace;"[140] and also further has, as I have stated, in his heart, the instinct or inspiration of "love," prompting him to do the right and loving thing to his Maker, and his fellowman.

If, then, he deliberately refuses to be guided by this "light," and trampling upon his instinctive love, chooses the wrong path, he certainly has committed a "sin" in thus "failing to do good;" and so, rightly, is both culpable before God, and has deteriorated in his own soul.

It therefore follows that "sin" is an act essentially of the will; and is merely relative to what might, and ought to have been done, in agreement with God's Cosmos — the "logoi" of His Logos,—and His inspired "light" and "love." The special harm, then, of sin consists in its disorder—a disorder that is disease in its progression; and in its fulfillment death (vide p. 66).

From this it follows that "sin" is an evil wrought, not only against God and His Cosmos, but also against ourselves; for, inasmuch as it transgresses the laws of our highest being—our intellect, our conscience, and our love,—it deteriorates, as I have just stated, our whole being, and slowly kills that Divine "image" in which we first were made. This is true from the fact that, as I have mentioned on p. 41 of my main treatise, a deliberate act of the will, or even a semi-conscious volition, establishes, at each repetition, a "habitual" character—a mental and moral groove,— in which, at last, the whole being becomes stereotyped and fixed. Every sinful choice, then, helps to form a "habitual" evil nature; and to deaden, and finally kill, the light and love in our souls; until, at last, the man has become an illogical and hateful fiend.

These considerations may help us to understand something of those abysms of evil—those "impersonal" and "unselfish" cruelties and hatreds,—to which I have already referred. Such acts, and states of mind certainly appear utterly irrational and inexplicable: but they are possibly conceivable if we consider them as the effects of a "habitual" preference for evil, and trampling upon love: coming, perhaps, by evil suggestion from devils; or perchance in some cases, even begotten by the man himself, out of the depths of his own evil-"habit:" irrational, such hatreds, and such preferences for evil, certainly are: but so (as I have already stated in my main treatise, p. 60) in its final completion, is *all* sin; for it must necessarily, by its very nature, be "illogical," or without the Logos and Wisdom of God.

Sin, then, we may finally say, in its essential character and nature, is the act of a finite will, deliberately, or "habitually"

---

(140) Vide pp. 42, 43.

choosing, against definite guidance and light, imperfection, or a wrong path of life: and furthermore; as it is against this guidance and light—this inspiration, from the Logos, of love and of truth,—it must needs be also against our love, and our reason, and contrary to our essential being itself; and partakes, therefore, of the character of an irrational hatred, corrupting and damning the soul.

From this it follows that redemption from this malignant and anti-logical disease can only come to the man by his own willing acceptance of an inspiration of "grace" and "love" from the Logos; or in other words, by his "free will" accepting, and co-operating with, precedent guidance and light: which redemption can only take the form of a union between the sinner and his God; which union, again, as I have endeavored, in my main treatise to show, was, and is effected by the Incarnation of our Lord, and by His Church, and her Sacraments depending on the same. Holiness, therefore, can only be a result, proceeding from such a Union with the Holy One; and never a mere antecedent state, preparatory to such a union.[141]

But to follow out these thoughts in all their fullness, and to illustrate their bearings upon the minutiae of ethics and theology, is, manifestly, beyond the design of this present Essay: my intention here being merely to expose and briefly refute, on the one hand, the materialistic conception of sin; and on the other, to give a slight sketch of the Catholic doctrine on the subject. This having now been accomplished, let us rapidly review the bearings of it all upon the doctrine of the Incarnation.

To begin, then, if "sin" were actually essential to the very being of Nature, and of man, as the Gnostics and the Puritans both supposed, then, evidently, Christ could not have become really Incarnate in this sinful flesh.

We would be driven, then, to predicate, either such a mere "simulacrum," or shell of humanity, as the Doketics, and (in a measure) Apollinarianism imagined; or else to think of our Lord, like Cerinthus and Nestorius did, as the "possession," or "inspiration" of the man Jesus by God. That is, of course, unless we escape either of these alternatives by making the Incarnation, in the fashion of Gess and Godet, such a "depotentiation" of the Logos as would make Him nothing but a sinner!

But if, again, we upheld this latter hypothesis, it would logically drive us to deny His Essential Godhead; and to conceive of Him, like the Arians did, not as the "Son," "$\delta\mu oo\acute{u}\sigma\iota o\varsigma$" with the Father; but as an *Emanation*, "$\dot{\epsilon}\tau\epsilon\rho o\acute{u}\sigma\iota o\varsigma$," and *deteriorated* from the Pure Absolute!

The Dualistic theory, then, that "sin" is an essential quality of Nature, and of man, is utterly and wholly incompatible with a

---

(141) Vide p. 72 and note 122. Nor, I might add, can it be the mere forensic "counting righteous" of an essentially impure and corrupt man.

true Incarnation of our Lord. Let us now see if the idea that "sin" is merely a "falling short," and nothing more (i. e. omitting any reference to our guidance from God), and essential, then, to a finite and ignorant creature, let us see, I repeat, if this idea is any more congruous than Dualism with the Catholic doctrine of the Incarnation.

I think not: for in such a case, obviously, Christ would either be very and true man; and therefore finite, as man; and therefore, again, *necessarily sinful;* or else we would be forced to think of Him as little more than the "quasi man" of the Doketics and Apollinarians.

But inasmuch as "sin" is, not a mere "falling short," but a "falling short in spite of, and in opposition to, inspired light and guidance," then, manifestly, Christ, while certainly a real man, and therefore properly limited and ignorant (vide Chap. V.), was yet, and in fact *could only be,* without sin; for He evidently could not transgress, or "fall short" of the inspiration and guidance from God, inasmuch as *He Himself was the Inspirer* (vide p. 45).

"Sin," then, because it is an imperfection, and a revolt against God, while possible to every finite will, is not an essential to such a will; and certainly is not predicable, in any sense, of the True and Perfect Man.

And finally: this consideration will expose the utter absurdity of the modern Unitarian contention that Christ, because He was a true, perfect, and representative man, must needs have been a sinner; and even that such faultiness is essential to His real sympathy with us!

For, as I need scarcely point out, this assertion is simply the reproduction of the Puritan dualistic theory, already exposed, of the evilness "per se" of the creature; and is as rational, to a theologian, as the claim that a perfect piece of porcelain, say, to be perfect, must needs be somewhere cracked, or mis-shapen!

But, manifestly, just the opposite fact holds true; for had our Blessed Lord been a sinner, He would not have been, as He is, "the Man," but could only have been a man alone; or in other words, would have utterly lost His representative manhood. For, obviously, had our Great Head, say, stolen, He could not adequately represent to God those of us who never stole; and so on through all the sins.

But a far more subtle, and dangerous fallacy lies in the claim that sin, or faultiness in our Head is essential to His real sympathy with us; for this vitally affects the doctrine of our Lord's High Priesthood, which, as I have stated in my main treatise (p. 70), is entirely dependent upon His human sympathy.

In refutation, then, of this specious contention we may point out that while *temptation,* and its concomitant, suffering, are certainly necessary to a sympathetic experience, yet *sin* assuredly is not; but, in accordance with what I have just stated, is utterly destructive of such sympathy, because destructive of corporate union and brotherhood. Sin, in brief, so far from making us more loving, merciful, sympathetic, and human, is, on the contrary, a mortal disease, destroying all love, mercy, and sympathy, corrupting and damning the soul, and making us, in short, as I have already shown, selfish, hateful, and inhuman fiends.

In no sense, therefore, is it at all proper, or predicable to Him, Who is our Elder Brother, Redeemer, and Priest—"the Friend of publicans and sinners,"—"in all points tempted like as we are, yet without sin."

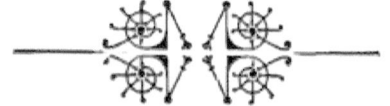

Spirit and Matter

THE question of the essential being of, and exact relation between "Spirit" and Matter," is a puzzle as old as philosophy, or even religion itself; and yet, in spite of all the thought, and all the discussion that have been spent upon it, it is still as fresh and absorbing as ever in its interest. And the reason for this perennial interest is not far to seek; for upon this essential being and inter-relation, depend many of the primary "data," both of our Philosophy and our Religion: the being of man, and the immortality of his soul—the existence of the Great Prime Cause, God, and His relation to the world—the origin, existence, and meaning of the vast Universe around us,—such are some of the all important issues, dependent for their solution on our answer to the above question.

The theories that attempt, in any degree, to answer this riddle may be roughly divided into three great classes; firstly, those that completely separate and divide the two worlds of "spirit," and of "matter," as did the Dualism of the Gnostics; secondly, those that identify all being as, simply and solely, different forms, or states of "matter," as did the atheistic Materialits of the last century; and thirdly, those that more or less fully identify all being, including "matter," as simply the forms, or products of "spirit," as do, in varying degrees, the Idealists, the Pantheists, Catholic theologians, and modern thinkers in general.

Of these three great classes, the first, or Dualistic theory, has been fairly well analysed and considered, and I trust, also confuted, in my Essay on the "Essential Nature of Sin;" but I may add to the arguments there advanced also the following: in the first place, not only is such a theory, by its conception of two utterly opposite and exclusive worlds—one of "spirit," and one of "matter,"—entirely incompatible with our instinctive intuitions, both of the unity of Nature, and the Unity of God, and also again of the Cosmical order of Creation, and its complete dependence upon Him,[142] not only, I say, is such a theory entirely incompatible with these primary intuitions, but it is, furthermore, totally contradicted, at every point, by our practical everyday observation.

For we are constantly experiencing the close inter-relations that exist between "spirit," or "mind," and "matter:" thus, phy-

---

[142] And, I might further add, is also opposed to the logical axiom mentioned in the Essay on "The Essential Nature of Sin" [p. 92], namely, that the opposite of an entity [in this case, God] cannot be another entity [as the Cosmos is], but only a *negation*.

sical phenomena, such as vibrations in the ether, are constantly being transmuted into mental experiences, such as "sight;" while, on the other hand, mental conditions, such as "anger," "fear," or "desire," are constantly becoming the originators of physical changes in our environment. And yet the only possible way in which Dualism can account for this close inter-relation is by predicating some such highly artificial theory of identical, yet entirely non-related movements in the two opposite worlds, as Descartes once put forward, in his theory of "animals as automata."

No! of a truth Dualism is utterly untenable in every respect; for, in the first place, it is primarily based (as I have shown in my previous Essay) upon a shallow and erroneous conception of "sin;" in the second place, it is opposed to all Religious and Philosophical axioms; and finally, it is contrary to all that we practically know of this world, and its component "matter."

But is the second theory of "spirit" and "matter"—i. e. the "material" one—any preferable? I think not. For if "spirit" be but another form of "matter," it evidently, then, must consist, like matter, of various combinations of those same "elemental atoms" that Materialism predicates as the sole realities of the Universe. Yet if this be true, then every "spirit," including our own "Ego," can be no such indivisible and individual unit, as we imagine; but can only be as temporary a compound, and therefore be also as destructible, as say the entity of water, or of wood.

But such an idea, I need hardly point out, contradicts the very foundations of all our knowledge, and experience; for the very first thing that I know, and in fact (as I will hereafter show), the *only* thing that I really *do* know, is that I exist and am *one*—an *individual*,—with powers of thought, and of will; all my "knowledge"—"practical," as well as "philosophical"—all my "experience," and my very existence itself, is ultimately based solely upon this primary fact; and no theory, therefore, and no reasoning can possibly overthrow it.

"But," says the Materialist, "this may all be true; and yet your 'primal intuitions' be false, and self delusive; for 'matter' is, and must be, all in all; and any separateness, then, or individuality, can be nothing more than a fanciful delusion."

To all this we may well reply by asking for the origin of this "fancy"—this "delusion;"—surely it is an axiom that things cannot be greater than their source, or in other words, cannot be without an adequate reason: if this be true, then how, may we not well ask, can physical atoms give rise to all the phenomena of thought; and especially to the "delusion" of individuality and non-materiality? Things, as we know them, do not turn against their causes in that way. And this argument, it will be noticed, applies equally as well to the "fiery nebula," predicated by Tyndall, in which he supposed was latent all the thought and life of the world, as it does to the crude Materialism of Cabanis.

But more than this: in thus giving the lie to our own primary intuitions, Materialism forfeits the very reason for its own existence; inasmuch as it was, and can only be intended as an attempted explanation of the various phenomena of life, and of the world. If, then, it denies, as contrary to its theory, our primal intuitions of truth, it both denies the very principles upon which everything is based; and also stands forth as a self confessed failure.

So much, then, for Materialism; a theory that can never attract the philosopher, or thoughtful man; and which, in fact, imperatively requires many "spiritual" and anti-materialistic conceptions —such as "laws," "causes," "life," and "reason,"—in order that it may be even intelligibly expressed.

We come now to the third theory, that, namely, which more or less fully identifies all being as simply either forms, or products of "spirit," and says that what we call "matter" is not "dead" at all; but is, on the contrary, the product of "life"—of "spirit;"—and has, in short, no possible existence, except as a phenomenon, or relation of that "life," or "spirit."

This theory, it will be noticed, is capable of a wide variety of expression. Thus it may be embodied in an extreme Idealistic form; and "matter" spoken of as simply the subjective phantasy of our own imagination.

But this, evidently, is well nigh as unreal and artificial an hypothesis as Materialism itself; for it is almost as absurd and self nugatory to deny our intuitions and sensations of an objective world, as it is to deny our own individual entity.

But again: it may also be formulated in a Pantheistic way; and both "spirit" and "matter" spoken of as being "merely phenomenal variations in the existence of the Absolute One."

To this the Christian philosopher answers that such a system again implies the falsity of our primal intuitions; for if all "matter" and all "spirit," including my own Ego and individuality, are nothing more than "phenomenal variations in the One;" and if I, with all else, have only a delusive sense of separation from "τὸ πᾶν;" then is all thought, all knowledge, and all logic and reasoning, including Pantheism itself, without any foundation in reality; and the "delusion of personality" is, besides, as inexplicable and causeless, as it is under the Materialistic scheme.

Then, finally, we have the theory of the Christian philosopher, who speaks of "spirit" and "matter," in the terms of our human knowledge and experience, not as things totally separate and opposite; nor yet, on the other hand, as entirely identical; but rather, if we may so express it, as two stages, or two aspects of the one creative act of God, by which He is ever giving existence to His world (vide p. 7).

"Spirit" and "matter," in short, under this conception, stand to one another in the Cosmos in much the same relation that they do in that "Micro-Cosmos"—the body and soul of man;—or in other words, "spirit" is conceived of, on the one hand, as being the creative and hypostatic "reality" of "matter;" and "matter" as being, on the other hand, the instrument, and phenomenal embodiment of an otherwise non-related, and therefore unknowable "spirit."[143]

And this, as I have just said, is speaking in the terms of our human knowledge and experience; for "matter," *as we know it*, at the ultimate analysis, is surely nothing else than an expression for a certain "catena of phenomena;" which phenomena, again, as I hope to show, are most probably the results, or products of "mind-will," or "spirit."

True, in vulgar phraseology, matter is sometimes spoken of as a "dead" something, in which certain qualities, or properties—such as "weight," "color," and "size"— essentially inhere; but this, I think, is simply an erroneous and vicious terminology, inherited from the dualistic, or quasi dualistic philosophy of the Greeks, and without any foundation in accurate thought.

For, looking at the subject calmly and clearly, no one, I think, will deny that all we know, and all we *can* know of matter is, simply and solely, this "catena of phenomena"—"color," "weight," "size," "smell," etc.,—or in other words, the various relations it may bear to us through our senses.

And even furthermore: our latest, and most accurate scientific knowledge testifies to the same fact, by assuring us that these same "phenomena," or "appearances," by which alone we apprehend "matter," are not, in any true sense, objective qualities residing *in* anything; but are rather *transient states, or waves of motion* in the unknown and unknowable "substratum;" which "waves," again, or "transient states," are translated by our "senses"—those sentinels of our mind and Ego—into entirely *subjectvei impressions*.

Thus, to illustrate, "sound," as we have discovered, is, simply and solely, wave pulsations in our atmosphere; and "color," and "light" are similar pulsations in the hypothetical "ether;" while "heat" is thought to be a vibration in the theoretical "molecules" themselves, conveyed probably by the same pulsations in the "ether" that also cause "light;" "weight," again, as we know, is simply an expression for the various attractions of "gravitation;" and finally, what we term "size," and "locality," is probably merely a synonymn for the larger, or smaller space within which these different forces are in action; so that scientifically speaking, "matter" is, as Huxley has well said, logically only our expression for a certain "vortex of forces," or in the above mentioned phrase, "catena of phenomena."

And in fact it is hard to see how it could well be otherwise; inasmuch as the nerves, in their various specialised forms of "optic,"

---

(143) Non-related and unknowable, that is, except to our "Hypostatic" Creator.

"aural," "tactual," etc., by which alone, as Physiology teaches, our brain (and, consequently, also our intellect, and our "Ego") communicates with the external world, could hardly receive, and convey to that brain, anything else than *motion;* and that, too, only in its transient variational state of *wave pulsations*.[144]

But yet, on the other hand, we must not overlook, or forget the fact that although the phenomenal relations of "matter," by which alone we know it, are, and must be, thus subjective; yet they are by no means such mere self delusions as the Idealistic school supposes. For although they are subjective impressions; yet nevertheless we did not, and in fact (as I will show) *could* not in any sense, *originate* them; but on the contrary, have merely *translated* them into that form, from impressions made upon us by something, or some change, that actually *is* in the external "non-Ego."

We have, I say, in the first place, by our senses, merely *translated* to ourselves some external occurrences. Thus, if we were without the power and capacity for "sight," there would, obviously, be *to us* no such thing as "color," or "light:" and furthermore; if, in the whole Universe, there was no eye, or at least no optic nerve, to "see," there would similarly be also no "light" that could be "seen." Yet nevertheless, the vibrations in the "ether," that we now know as "light," would certainly not thereby cease to be; and might, possibly, even impress themselves upon the various sensitive beings of the Universe (including ourselves) by some other sense that that of "sight."[145]

In fact we are far too apt to think of our five[146] senses, by the means of which we are put into cognisable relation with our environment, as the only possible relation to that environment that

---

(144) Only, I say, in its transient variational state; for a constant and unvarying force (as, for example, the pressure of the atmosphere) would, manifestly, be *undifferentiated* to the senses; and they, consequently, would be totally passive to its existence; we would, and must, therefore, be entirely and absolutely ignorant of such a force: except, indeed, as our reason might require it as the theoretical "substratum" of sensible variations.

Thus, in the instance given of the pressure of the atmosphere, this is, as we know, entirely outside of our senses; and therefore wholly unknown to us; *except* in its variational form of a wind; or except, again, as the theoretical cause of barometrical pressure; which latter, still further, is known to us only by reason of a "variation" artificially introduced, namely, a vacuum.

And so, again, is the "ether," if there be such a thing, wholly unknown, and unknowable to us; except as the theoretical "substratum" of certain "variational wave pulsations"—namely, "heat" and "light."

All this may help us to understand why a *constant* phenomenon, such as the ticking of a clock, soon ceases to impress us; for the "variations" have become regular; and therefore partake of the character of a constant force. But let that ticking suddenly cease—let there be, in other words, a "variation" in the "variations,"—and our nerves are at once impressed, and we are startled, even from the soundest sleep.

And this "variational law" of the senses depends, I think, on the primary law that "knowledge" imperatively requires, first, "appreciation," then "synthesis" or correlation, and lastly "analysis" or differentiation and comparison; and this last stage is absolutely necessary before a fact can be "known." "Variations," then, are indispensable to "knowledge" acquired through the senses; inasmuch as they are required for both the "differentiation," and the "comparison."

(145) As, in fact, they probably do impress themselves now in the phenomenon of "heat."

(146) Or possibly *six;* inasmuch as some Physiologists differentiate between the senses of "touch" and of "weight." But yet the exact number does not affect my argument.

there can be; and of the information that they convey to us, as the only possible information there is; and in brief, of what we sensuously learn and "know," as absolute and final truth.

Yet surely it is quite conceivable that there should be a being who should possess, not five, but five hundred senses; not one of whom should be at all similar to any of ours. In such a case, obviously, that being could not "see," or "hear," or "smell" as we do; yet nevertheless those innumerable forces, and changes in the Cosmos, that we, in some small measure, so dimly apprehend, would doubtless be far more freely and widely apprehended by those five hundred varieties of sensitive nerves, conveying a larger information concerning those changes, than we can know, to the sensible being to whom they belonged.

It follows, then, that our "senses" are, as I have said, merely the translations to us of some change, or some occurrence, that actually *is* in the external "non-Ego;" and this brings me to my second point, namely the *objective* origin in *reality* of these *subjective* phenomena.

And to begin, I may say that the very fact that they are *wave pulsations*, which we only *partially* apprehend, and *translate*, is, in itself, plain evidence of this external origin; for if they were mere self hallucinations, they would not, obviously, be *partial translations* at all, but *complete originals;* nor would they, again, in such a case, partake of their unforeseen, and (so to speak) arbitrary pulsational character; but would, on the contrary, be both *anticipated*, and *constant;* and yet, as I have just shown, it is entirely upon this unexpected and "variational wave" character that their whole cognisability depends. It is plainly evident, therefore, from these considerations, that the origin of these phenomena must be external to us; or in other words, that they must have, as their creative "substratum," a real, and not merely ideal existence.

Nor can their transitional character be objected against this reality; for while the occurrences that they represent to us may be, and in fact, as I have shown, must be thus transitory and fleeting; yet nevertheless, *while they exist*, they are, none the less, actual and real: a changing cloud, while it lasts, is as "real" as a granite rock; and the rock, again, while it lasts, has as true a relation to the Universe as, say, an archangel of God.

"Matter," then, although it may be, and is, only a phenomenal relation, has yet, for its hypostatic origin and "substratum," as true an actual and objective existence as anything can have: this is, evidently, a most important fact; and one that should be strongly impressed on the mind; for upon it, as I will hereafter show,[147] most important issues depend.

But yet, of this actual and hypostatic cause and origin of the phenomena of "matter"—this "noumenal" being, or actual nature

---

(147) Vide the Essay on "the Primary Criterion of Truth."

as it is "in itself,"—we, not being its Creators and Upholders, must be entirely ignorant: and the only probable, or indeed, as I will endeavor to show, possibly coherent idea we can form of it, is in the terms of our human knowledge and experience; by saying that the creative and hypostatic "cause" of all the phenomena known to us as "matter," is simply "life," "mind-will," or "spirit;" even as the "cause" (and the *only* "cause," too, in the whole Universe, that we actually "*know*") of the phenomenal "matter" of our bodies is our own "life" and "mind-will"—our creative and hypostatic "spirit," or "Ego."

And this being of ours can, perhaps, be most accurately summarised as follows: we are, first, a living existence, possessed of the essential powers of (1) autonomous will, (2) thought, and (3) self consciousness: and let it be noted that in this progression, each power, or faculty imperatively requires its precedent faculty; "self consciousness," presupposing "thought;" and "thought" a "will."[148]

But while this is the theoretical and "a priori" order, our practical appreciation of that order (inasmuch as we are not our own creators) must, obviously, be in the reverse direction—namely "a posteriori," or inductive;—or in other words, I must, necessarily, first realize my own self consciousness; then my thinking powers, upon which that self consciousness is based; and finally, my power of autonomous will, that underlies all, and is the central core, and essential mark of differentiation, of my Ego itself.

The first thing, therefore, that I recognise, and the very first that I can recognise, is my own self consciousness: but this realisation, again, necessarily implies two sets of relations, one "internal," and the other "external."

First, then, an "internal" set of relations is implied, namely a *triune* self relationship; for *I* (the thinking subject) am conscious that *I* (as an "object") exist; and am, further, *conscious* of the consciousness;[149] and this triune self relationship is absolutely essential to all subsequent rational knowledge.

But inseparably interlinked with, and inter-dependent upon, this consciousness of self, is also the consciousness of an external world; for, surely, if there were no such realization of an external "non-Ego," there could be no comparison, and differentiation; and, consequently, no possibility of "knowledge."

I am conscious, then, both of a triune self, and of an external world; and am thereby assured that I am an individual; and possess the faculties of "thought" (in its three-fold variations of "reason," "conscience," and "love"), and of "will," together with

---

(148) Or, in other words, the "power of choice." For, obviously, without this faculty the analysis of "thought" could not take place.
(149) All, I believe, will readily grant the first two of these relations—namely, the "Ego" as both "subject" and "object;"—and that the third step for the realisation of this relation] is also indispensable to "self-consciousness," is, I think, evident from the fact that without such a realisation, the subjectivity of the mind never rises above self-delusion; as in the case of madmen, or of dreams.

a sensitive nervous "body," linking those internal faculties with an external world.

And having such a nature, I can, therefore, in my internal relations, reason, and know truth, know good and evil, and feel love, joy, anger, and hatred; I can originate motion, and decide (within certain broad limits) my own actions; and in my external relations, can both experience, through my sensitive nerves, a variety of sensations (such as heat, cold, weight, light, etc.); and can also, as I will show, translate to myself these sensations; thus correlating these two sets of relations—the internal, and the external—the one with the other.

I am, then, given the knowledge of two inter-connected sets of relations, or "worlds"—one of them internal, mental, "Egoistic," and "spiritual;" and the other external, bodily, "non-Egoistic," and "material;"—and from the first of these worlds (or the "spiritual" one), I get the ideas of various "spiritual" relations,—such as "cause, and effect" (from my will), "logical order, and law" (from my reason), "loveliness and hatefulness" (from my emotions), and "holiness, and sin" (from my conscience);—while, on the other hand, from my "external," or "material" world, I get the conception of an external "non-Ego" of "matter," with its phenomenal relations of "heat," "weight," "color," "size," etc.

And furthermore: it is in this latter "world" of the external "non-Ego" that I must class, as a general rule, even my own body; for although it is certainly mine; yet nevertheless, as I sensuously apprehend it (i. e. by touch, sight, and smell, etc.), it is, evidently, nothing else, practically, than the external, and objective "cause" of a "subjective catena of phenomenal relations" to its own nerves; being thus (if we may so express it), like the mind, "self conscious"—or in other words, apprehending (as a "subject") itself (as an "object"); and thirdly, realising that "auto-apprehension."—But yet further: I not only "know" my body thus sensuously and "externally," but also actually and "internally" (although, it is true, in a somewhat dim and imperfect manner) as the creation of my "Ego," and under my guidance and sway—know it, in other words, not only in its "phenomenal relations," but also (in a measure) "really," and as its "hypostatic cause" (i. e. my own individuality) is "in itself." Here, then, is that synchronising point of my "material" and "spiritual" worlds, by which I am enabled to make that necessary translation and correlation to which I have already alluded.

But still further: I have this knowledge of these two differentiated, yet closely interconnected and interdependent "worlds" —one internal, "Egoistic," and "spiritual," the other external, "non-Egoistic," and "material:" — but in this last mentioned world—i. e. the "external"—I again perceive differences. In the ultimate sense, it is true, *all* of its phenomena appeal to my "spiritual world," through my senses (by reason of the synchronisms obtained through my body), and give me the impressions of "order," "reason," and "beauty;" such appeal being, in fact, the only means by which I can logically and coherently translate to myself those sensuous impressions. But although *all* the external phenomena make this spiritual appeal; yet *some* make it in a more striking and vivid way than others; so that in interpreting them, I cannot but project myself, to a greater or less degree, into them; and think of their creative and hypostatic "cause" as, more or less, such a one as myself.

Thus, if the observed phenomena be, in all respects, similar to my own, I think of that "cause" as another man; but if the similarity be only partial, then I conceive of the "cause" as a conscious, and "willing" living animal; or as an unconscious, and "non-willing" living plant; or finally, as a non-living, and merely "material" stock, or stone, according to the measure and degree of identity.

In short, when we try to interpret to ourselves and "know" this external Universe around us, we cannot but think of it and translate it in terms of our own self conscious being, and of that synchronism in our body, spoken of above; and although we may add to our stock of conceptions by experience, and the study of the Cosmos; yet even these extra conceptions are, and must be, themselves ultimately based on the prime factors of our own existence, and its self conscious and intuitional or essential knowledge.

We cannot, then, be aught but "anthropometric," and read all things through the medium, and in the terms of our own individuality; for although our "knowledge," even of the depths of our own being, and certainly, then, also of the external Cosmos, as read through that being, is exceedingly limited, partial, and relative; yet inasmuch as it is, obviously, all that we possess, we cannot, manifestly, get either beyond, or behind it—cannot, in other words, think external, and superior to ourselves;—but must, necessarily, accept it as true, at least relatively, and as far as it goes.

When, therefore, we turn to what is called "merely material" substance—i. e. something whose phenomenal relations to us we can interpret only (or at least, most evidently) in terms of our own "material" body, such as "color," "weight," "size," etc.,—are we not abundantly justified in predicating as the Ultimate Creative and Hypostatic "Cause" of that "matter" something similar to the only hypostatic and creative "cause" of phenomena that we know, namely our own "Ego," "spirit," or "mind will?" And we have all the more warrant for this comparison in the "spiritual" effects—such as "design," "beauty," "law," etc.,— that we may observe in "matter," if we will but look for them. Above I have defined "mere matter" as something whose phenomenal relations to us we can at least most evidently interpret in the terms of our own bodily existence; but yet, as I have again stated, even "mere matter" must have its mental and "spiritual" relations—like "design," "beauty," and "law"—if it is to be coherent, and therefore intelligible: if this were not true—if all the Universe, including "mere matter," were not a logical Cosmos,—then, obviously, our environment would be as unintelligible as a child's chance heap of alphabet blocks; "knowledge" would be unobtainable; and life, in brief, not possible. But, as we know, the Universe, including its component "matter," is intelligible—is a *Cosmos;*—and we, therefore, can "know" things, and their "laws;" and therefore, again, can exist. This thought I have already touched upon in my main treatise, in the exposition of the Immanence of the Logos (vide p. 1 et seq.); but the point I am now insisting upon is merely that there is this plain evidence of a mental and "spiritual" sway over "matter;" a sway that is, in fact, as essential and necessary to the very being of that "matter," as the innate qualities of "volition" and "thought" are to our own existence.

This being so, then we are, surely, abundantly justified in saying that all "matter" is, and can only be, like our bodies, the phenomenal creation of a hypostatic "life," "mind will," or "spirit;" and that not only where such a "cause" is allowed by all, namely in the case of our fellowmen, and (in their degree) animals, and even plants; but also in relation to that "purely material world"—the stocks, and the stones,—whose Great Hypostatic Creator and Sustainer, the savage, with his pantheistic fetichism, dimly apprehends; and we, Christian philosophers, who have been enlightened by the Incarnation, more fully and accurately apprehend, as the Omnipresent and Omnipotent Lord and Giver of Life, Who Eternally Proceedeth from the "'Αρχή" of the Father, through the Eternal Logos of God.

But, it may be objected, is there not one serious flaw in this argument? No doubt it is true that the only conceivable Ultimate Prime Cause of the various phenomena we know as "matter" is, and can only be "Mind Will," or "Spirit." But, it may be, and in fact, is asked, what right have we to predicate to that "Mind Will" *self consciousness*, or in other words, *personality;* may it not rather be thought of as the "Absolute Unconscious" of Schopenhaur and Hartmann? For is not "life"—that creative hypostasis of "matter,"—in even the majority of its manifestations, utterly unconscious and blind? This, for instance, is its character in plants; and it is little less so in the myriad lower forms of animal life—animalculae, and molluscs;—while, as we rise in the scale of being, it is, in the higher animals, still very limited (so far as we can judge) in its self realisation; and even in man — the creature who is, to a special degree, the "self conscious"—there are still vast tracts in his nature—aye! in the very citadel of "self consciousness" itself, namely the mind, and its memories—that are entirely outside of his self realisation.

This being so, then by what right, it is asked, do we predicate to the Ultimate and Absolute, that (namely "self consciousness") which is the property of life in only a few instances; and even then, and at its best, only to an imperfect degree?

To this it may be replied that we are abundantly justified in predicating the Absolute—the Creator and Sustainer—as, at the very least, a Self conscious Person: for, in the first place, He is not the mere Pantheistic sum of "$\tau o\ \pi \tilde{a} \nu$;" but, on the contrary, is Transcendent over His creation, because Immanent in it:[150] and in the second place, we surely cannot but predicate to the Ultimate the possession of at least the highest powers and qualities to which He gives existence in His Creatures.

Thus He gives "being" to "mere matter," because He is the Supreme Being; and trees, and the lower animals have "life" from Him, because He is the Eternal Life; to the higher animals, again, He gives a "willing life," because He is the Omnipotent Willer; and finally, man possesses both "will," and "thought" (with its triune faculties of "reason," "conscience," and "love"), with a resultant more or less perfect "self consciousness," because, and only because, he is given such essential being and existence by the inspiration of Him Who is Ever the True, the Holy, and the Loving Willer: in short, we cannot, as I have said, but predicate to the Absolute the full possession of at least the perfections to which He gives existence in us.

The *perfections*, I say; and this, of course, at once exposes the sophistry of predicating Him as the "Unconscious," because He gives, say to trees, unconscious life; for what He gives is life; and its "unconsciousness" is, in no sense, a positive, but is rather a negative quality.[151] And this consideration, again, also cuts away any argument as to the Absolute being unholy and evil, or at least, "non-holy," because evil is found in His world; for, as I have shown in the previous Essay on "the Essential Nature of Sin," "evil," in its concrete state of "evil acts," or "sin," is, at the last analysis, nothing more than a negation of the good, and a falling short of God's Inspirational guidance; and therefore does not proceed from Him.

And as a further argument for our contention that the Ultimate "Mind Will," or "Spirit" is, not the "Unconscious," but the Supreme Person, we may well inquire what possible conception can be formed of a Perfect Mind and Reason that is not, at the same time, Self conscious?

---

(150) Vide p. 11 of the main treatise.
(151) As well might we argue that a watchmaker could have no more perfections than those that belong to his watch. For while he must possess *at least* the positive qualities of his creation—namely, its ingenuity, and the thoughts of measurement and of time expressed in it;—yet he surely is not *limited* by its wants—i. e. of life, of conscience, or of reason:—nay! it might better be argued that he must have far more than he has given, or could give to his creation.

True it is that "will," as I have already stated, may not always realise its own activity; and even the mind, again, on occasions, as in dreams, and "unconscious cerebration," may not fully appreciate its own reasoning: nevertheless the logical crown and completion of both "will," and "reason" is, I insist, a self realisation and self consciousness. In fact, as I have previously stated (vide p. 103), the necessary order and progression seems to be first "will," then "thought," and finally "self consciousness," with its triune self relation, and its realisation of the external "non-Ego;" and it is not until this progression has been fulfilled that "knowledge," and especially its resultant—"wisdom"—is practicable to the mind.

And yet again: may not this phenomenon of "unconscious thought and will" be best explicable as the activities of the Inspiring Logos in our souls? For from that Enlightening Logos, as I have shown,[152] come all the necessary "prime data" of "reason," "conscience," and "love" that make our existence possible: and these inspired "data" are, surely, essentially *subconscious* in their nature; inasmuch as they are (so to speak) the "foundation strata" of our very being; which only "out-crop," and rise to the light, in our very partial self realisation.

If this be true, then may we not insist that "self consciousness" actually is (as it certainly abstractly appears to be) absolutely necessary to, and inseparable from "thought" and "will;" the only apparent exceptions—namely, in the instances above mentioned—being only apparent, and not real; inasmuch as the "blind thought and will," of which we occasionally catch a glimpse in our own personality, are, properly speaking, *not ours at all;* but belong rather to that Hypostatic Logos, Who is ever Inspiring us, and giving us *existence*; so that this "thought and will" then, are, actually, not "unconscious" at all; but rise to absolute self realisation in Him.

And finally, may we not point out that the predication of the Absolute as "Unconscious Thought," and especially as "Unconscious Will," would, practically, be nothing else than predicating Him as *"Blind Chance!"* For surely a "will" without wisdom, or logical plan (both of which certainly imply self consciousness) is nothing else than an illogical and fortuitous "force;" and such a "Prime Cause" is clearly untenable from all the laws of thought and experience—religious, philosophical, or scientific.

This being the case, then surely we can but predicate to the Creative Wisdom all that we mean by "personality." True, it might be objected that while there doubtless is, in the Absolute, the triune state of self knowledge—i. e. in the Blessed Trinity of Father, Son, and Holy Spirit;—yet the second prerequisite to a full "Personality" is wanting, namely the realisation of an

---

(152) Vide pp. 2, 42, 43, and note 1 of my main treatise.

external "non-Ego," inasmuch as He is Immanent in all. Nevertheless this would lead us, not to a "Mind Will" that was *inferior* in its self consciousness to man, but rather to a Consciousness that is *super-eminent* above ours; such as, in fact, we cannot anthropometrically picture, or conceive.

And yet further; while the Absolute is certainly Immanent in all, yet is not the Cosmos, by its very being, in some real sense, a "non-Ego" to Him; inasmuch as He has given, and is ever giving to it a real and true existence? (vide p. 7). Here, manifestly, we are sounding the very abysms of being; and human thoughts and conceptions fail us: but yet we are, surely, abundantly justified in saying that He Who is our Creator, and the Hypostatic Reality of the Universe around us, has at least Personality, if not something higher.

But it may be finally objected to all the above that this is a mere delusive projection of ourselves and our being into Nature: and what warrant, it may be asked, have we for thus making ourselves the measure of all things?

Well, if by "making ourselves the measure" is meant the anthropomorphically giving to the Ultimate our finite limitations, then, obviously, such a course is absurd. But if an anthropometric interpretation of all things is objected to, and the predication of the Absolute in the terms of our *perfections*, then how, it may well be asked, can we do otherwise? Surely we are quite warranted, by every canon of thought, in thus predicating to the Absolute *at least* all our perfections in their supremest degree; so long, of course, as we are careful not to limit Him to these perfections *alone*. This is not, in any sense, making Him a man; but is merely thinking of Him as men must think.

And finally, if the correctness and validity of even our most perfect conceptions are themselves called in question, we can only reply that such a cavil is self nugatory and untenable; inasmuch as we cannot but hold, as thoroughly valid and impregnable, our necessary ideas: but the full discussion of this point must be reversed for another Essay.[153]

"Matter," then, to sum up all our previous discussion, is simply our name for a certain catena of variational phenomena ,"subjectively" translated to us by our senses, yet "objectively" originating outside of ourselves; and that "objective origin"—that hypostatic cause—we can, as I have shown, only coherently picture to ourselves as "life," "mind will," or "spirit;" which "spirit," again, we can, in some cases, recognise as belonging to beings who are either similar, or inferior to ourselves—such as other men, animals, or plants;—but which, in the great majority of instances, such as in reference to the "merely material" Universe around us, or even the prime origin of those beings—men, ani-

---

(153) **Vide** the Essay on "the Primary Criterion of Truth."

mals, and plants—to which I have just referred, we can only predicate as the Omnipresent and Omnipotent Prime Cause of all things—the Lord and Giver of Life,—Who both creates, and ever upholds the Cosmos; and Who, possessing at least all the Plenitude of Wisdom, Holiness, Love, and Power, is a Perfect Self conscious Person; unless, indeed, He can be better thought of (if only we could conceive such a thing) as "Hyper-Personal."

"Matter," then, is solely the product, or creation of "spirit"—of secondary and created spirits, or ultimately of the Great Prime Spirit;—and the world is therefore (to employ a daring phrase) the "body" of the Infinite God.

But yet, on the other hand, since it is this product, or creation of "spirit," it is also its necessary embodiment; at least in its finite relations. In fact, so far as we can judge from our own experience and reason, a "spirit," stripped of its raiment of "matter," would be both absolutely helpless, and entirely unknown and unknowable, except to its Creator and God: this thought I have already touched upon in my main treatise, with reference to the "descent into Hell." And this unknowableness, and non-relation of a disembodied spirit is evident, I think, from the following considerations: if, on the one hand, a "spirit" could both work its will upon, and make itself known unto other entities; then it would, obviously, be in a phenomenal (and therefore *material*) relation to such entities; or would, in other words possess a "body:" while, on the other hand, if it were without such *phenomenal* relations, then it would, obviously, be without any relation at all; unless, in truth, it be with its own Hypostatic Prime Creator and Upholder—God;—and possibly, then, through Him, with other entities.

But not only does this law that a "body" or "matter" implies "relation," and "relation" implies a "body," hold good with respect to our own "Ego," but it certainly seems to me to be also valid with respect to the Great Prime "Ego" Himself, namely the Creator. For, evidently, so long as He gave no existence to the Cosmos, He was utterly unknown and unknowable; and even now that He has given it such existence, He, in His own Essence, is, and must be, entirely unknowable, not only to man, but to the whole of Creation; and can only be even faintly apprehended, and known to be, first "materially" and "sensuously" (so to speak), as the Hypostatic Cause of the Cosmos; and secondly, again "materially" and "sensuously," as the God-man Who was Incarnate among us; and finally, can also, perhaps, be indefinitely apprehended by us, as our Prime "Hypostasis" and Creator; which last relation is a "non-sensuous" and "non-material" one, only because it is creative and direct.

"Spirit," then, we can say is the necessary hypostatic "Cause" of "matter;" and "matter" is its necessary embodiment, and thing that is caused. This is a hypothesis that, as I think I have shown, follows the strictest lines of thought; and while it gives rise, I believe, to no serious difficulties, or self contradictions, at the same time solves, or at least gives us the clue to solving, all that we can hope to comprehend. And while, again, it fully expresses all the portions of truth that are contained in the clashing systems of Dualism, Materialism, Idealism, and Pantheism, yet it carefully avoids all their mistakes, and falls into none of their errors.

Thus, with Dualism, it acknowledges the separateness of the spheres of "spirit" and "matter;" while yet their illogical and untenable opposition is denied: and so again, it sees, with Materialism, the practical and true reality of "matter," and its close interconnection with "spirit;" but yet does not suicidically depict it as the only reality and existence: then, with Idealism, the entirely "subjective" character of our sensuous impressions of "matter" is realised; while yet the vital fact is also recognised that these "subjective impressions" are, in no sense, mere hallucinations; but have an origin in "objective reality:" and finally, while it appreciates, with Pantheism, the grand truth of the Unity of all things, and their inherence in God; yet it does not, like Pantheism, make the fatal mistake of calling that unity a confusion, and our sense of separateness and individuality a delusion; but on the contrary, recognises the axioms that the Immanence of God implies also His Transcendence, that our sense of individuality is, and must be valid, and in short, that "differentiation in unity" is the primary law, not only of knowledge, but of life, and the Cosmos itself.

There is yet one more point that should be touched upon, and that is the precise character, under this hypothesis, of the interaction that there is between "spirit" and "matter;" inasmuch as both are in fact, as our daily experience assures us, so interacting and inter-connected.

Well, as to the action of "spirit" on "matter," that, as I have just laid down, is "hypostatic" and creative. And as to the opposite action, that, namely, of "matter" on "spirit," this we can, possibly, best conceive of as "influential," or "inductive" (so to speak) in its character; inasmuch as it operates by changing the environing relations of that spirit; and thus causing it to act. This seems to me to fairly represent all the action and influence that "matter" has upon "spirit."

And finally we may briefly view the bearings of all this on the Catholic doctrine of the Incarnation. One such bearing I have already touched upon, when I stated that this manifestation to man was the second (and as I may further add, the clearest) way by which God is "sensuously," or "materially" known to man. To this consideration we may also add the following: if "spirit" and "matter" were so entirely separate and opposed, as the Dualists imagined, then, manifestly, God could not have assumed a body;

but could only have been, either such a phantasy, as the Doketics, in fact, pictured; or else such a mere inspiration in a man, as Cerinthus, and later, Nestorius supposed: and so again, if "matter" were all there is, as the Materialists say, then, obviously, there would be no Logos to be Incarnate: but on the other hand, if "spirit" alone exists, and "matter" is only our subjective illusion, as the Idealists maintain, then evidently we again could have only a Doketic Christ: while finally, if God be merely the sum of all force, and all being—or is, in other words, merely our expression for "$\tau o\ \pi \tilde{a} \nu$"— and Pantheism the true Philosophy; then, manifestly, an Incarnation would be both meaningless and impossible.

But since "spirit" and "matter" are both of them actual and dissimilar entities; and yet also entities that are closely interconnected, inasmuch as they stand to one another as do a "hypostasis" and its creation—a "cause" and its "effect;"—and since, again, both ultimately derive their existence from Him, Who is the Ultimate Cause of all; then, evidently, the Logos, Who is that "Immanent Hypostasis"could become truly Incarnate and Very Man; and that, not by joining Himself to a separate humanity, but by creating around Him a real humanity—mind, bodily life and body :— which humanity, again, because created and upheld by Him, could, obviously, not exist a moment apart from Him; but was "hypostatically" one with Him, and "never to be divided."

The Primary Criterion of Truth

THERE is one double assumption that has been made in the preceding pages, which few, I imagine, of my readers, will be disposed to cavil at; and that is, first, that our senses are trustworthy and reliable, at least as far as they go; and secondly and especially, that the instinctive, or innate "prime data"—mathematical, logical, moral, etc.,—by which we both think, and interpret to ourselves the information that is given us by our senses, that these "prime data," I say, are also correct and entirely valid, again at least as far as they go; and in brief, that we are in a true relation to the Cosmos; and are both able to know, and (according to our finite capacity) actually do know, the facts concerning that Cosmos.

These primary assumptions, as I have said, probably few will call in question; nevertheless both for the sake of the few who may dispute these premises, and also to ensure a logical completeness to our arguments, it may, perhaps, be well for us to see if these assumptions can be defended.

For there have been those in all ages who have raised this initial question of Philosophy; and asked, like Pilate, "what is truth?" We have a sensuous appreciation of the world; and we, necessarily, form practical theories and ideas, concerning that world, and its "facts:" but, say these questioners, what possible assurance, or even reasonable probability have we that these things *are* "facts;" or in other words, what certainty have we that there is any correlation, or analogy whatever between the Cosmos as we *imagine* it to be, and the Cosmos as it really *is?*

This is, evidently, a most serious question, and one that strikes to the very foundation of all our philosophy, all our science, all our thought, and even our very existence itself; inasmuch as upon the answer that we return, depends our whole attitude towards our God, His world, and our daily life. For if we decide that we do not know reality—that we are, in other words, self deluded by our thought and senses,—or even that we are unable to know if we be not so deluded, then obviously we must sink into pessimism, apathy, and despair.

But if, on the other hand, we can answer that both our senses, and our reasoning faculties are entirely valid, and both put us into actual relations with the Cosmos, and give us, if not final and absolute, at least such relative truth as we can finitely apprehend, if such, I say, be our answer, then, evidently, we can face our life and its problems in a hearty and common sense fashion, trusting in our Creative Father, His guidance, and His love. Such, then, are the two alternatives.

To solve this riddle it is evident that we must first decide upon the validity of our "prime data;" inasmuch as upon these "prime data" depends the whole of our being. And the first point that we can make is that they must be accepted as thus valid; for we can get neither beyond, nor behind them. And furthermore; the only possible way in which we could even guess at their falsity, would be by their illogically contradicting themselves; but this, as a matter of fact, we know they do not do: and in truth, if they were so self nugatory, they could not possibly endure; but would speedily destroy both themselves and us: and this brings me to an all conclusive argument.

When we gaze upon the Cosmos in which we live, we necessarily think of it, and treat it, as I have already said (vide p. 106) not as a child's chance heap of alphabet blocks—a "fortuitous concourse of atoms,"—but as a logical and coherent volume—a logical Cosmos, upheld by the Logos—which we, as logical beings, made in the "image" of that Logos, are able to logically and accurately apprehend: it is this fact, as I have repeatedly pointed out, and this fact alone, that makes, not only our science, or our thought, but even our mere animal existence possible.

But let this not be true, let us, in other words, be "self hallucinated" by our "prime data" and our senses, and at "cross purposes" with the Universe, then it is surely obvious that the said Universe would speedily crush us out of existence. This, as I have said, is an all conclusive argument, from which there is no escape.

But, says the Pessimistic Nihilist, although all this may be true, and granting that our "innate ideas of truth"—our "prime data,"—are, and must be thus valid, yet may we not, at the same time, be deceived by the testimonies of our senses? For these "senses," as every student knows, are only our "subjective" and personal impressions; may they not, then, be also delusions? And if they be so delusive, then although we may have valid truth in ourselves, yet how can we know it in the Cosmos; inasmuch as we are not in a true relation to that Cosmos?

This is, evidently, a most specious and subtle objection; and yet the same argument, namely that of practical efficiency, and even existence, that establishes the validity of our "prime data," is equally available here. For if our senses be mere delusions, then how do either those senses continue, or we, their possessors, practically exist? Under such a hypothesis, a blind man walking on the edge of a precipice, would not be in greater peril than we; and speedy catastrophy and extinction would be inevitable!

But the best reply, I think, lies in pointing out that, as I have laid down in my Essay on "Spirit and Matter," while our "senses" it is true, do give us, and can only give us entirely *subjective* impressions; yet these impressions are, in no sense, self originated and delusive; but are, in every instance, *representations* and *translations* to us of *objective* and *external* realities. Any "subjective" hallucination, then, is, manifestly, out of the question; and our sensuous appreciation of things, while necessarily far from being perfect and absolute, is yet entirely accurate, relatively, at least, and as far as it goes.

Yet it may be again asked, do not our senses, as a fact, occasionally deceive us? Do we not hear, and see things falsely—see the sun move around the earth, or hear a ventriloquist "throw his voice;"—and are there not, again, such things as the apparitions of madness, or delirium: and if our senses can so deceive us in some particulars, then why not in all?

The answer to this lies in the accurate discrimination between a "deception by our senses," which possibility I deny, and a "deception by our false *interpretation* of those senses," which possibility we must allow. In other words, what our senses give us are, as I have shown, merely the impressions or "translations" of external phenomena; and we, guided, first by our intuitional "prime data," and secondly by our practical experience, derived from former phenomenal impressions (and ultimately based, then, on our "intuitional data"), guided, I say, by these "prime data," made more effective by experience, we proceed to interpret to ourselves the aforesaid "phenomenal impressions," as originating from certain external entities. And in these two guides to our interpretation—namely "prime data," and experience—while the first, being primary, is infallible (or at least, incontrovertible), yet the second, being secondary, and variously derived, has by no means this character, but is exceeding liable to mislead.

Thus, to illustrate; we have been accustomed to connect a certain roar with a lion; and when an ostrich gives a similar roar, we again think it is a lion; and then say, perhaps, that "our senses have deceived us." But this is not really the case, for what our senses told us concerning the roar, and also in connection with the instances, mentioned above, of the sun, and the ventriloquist, was entirely accurate, at least so far as it concerned those senses; and the fault of our mistakes lay wholly in our hasty conclusions from insufficient premises.

As to the phenomena of mental aberrations. the subject is too little known for us to dogmatise: but yet it is. I think, evident that it is not the senses that are here at fault; but rather the inchoate and illogical dreamings of a disordered mind.

Both our "primal intuitions of truth," and the information concerning the "non-Ego" given us by our senses, are, then, entirely valid and reliable; and we are therefore labouring under no nightmare of self hallucination; but can and do know truth, and the Cosmos as it actually is, at least relatively to our finite intelligences.

The only source, then, of possible error lies, as I have said, in our interpretation of those senses; and this element of uncertainty in our knowledge, and liability to error, has, probably, the same reason for its existence as has temptation (vide p. 40 et seq.): for it must primarily, and necessarily, spring from our finite self existence, and want of Omniscience; and is necessary, in the second place, for our proper education.

One vital fact, then, that we should ever remember, is that this truth and knowledge of ours is entirely relative and partial. Some people are ever insisting upon the necessity for Absolute Truth; as if, indeed, that could be known by any being, other than the Absolute Himself. Yet assuredly "Absolute Truth" is all comprehensive—is all that is;—and cannot, therefore, be apprehended by any finite mind: all that we can do is to relatively apprehend truth in sections (so to speak); and at the same time, recognise it as relative. Our God has given us but a finite existence; and we can, therefore, but "know" and "prophesy in part;" and follow as closely as we can the guidings of Him Who is the Inspiring Logos in our souls; and Who has been further manifested to us as the Christ.

www.ingramcontent.com/pod-product-compliance
Lightning Source LLC
Chambersburg PA
CBHW022139160426
43197CB00009B/1348